The Mirage of Power

FOREIGN POLICIES OF THE GREAT POWERS
Edited by C. J. Lowe

The Reluctant Imperialists   C. J. Lowe

Vol. I British Foreign Policy 1878–1902
Vol. II The Documents

The Mirage of Power   C. J. Lowe and M. L. Dockrill

Vol. I British Foreign Policy 1902–14
Vol. II British Foreign Policy 1914–22
Vol. III The Documents

*From Sadowa to Sarajevo: The Foreign Policy
of Austria–Hungary, 1866–1914*   F. R. Bridge

The Mirage of Power

volume one

British Foreign Policy 1902-14

C. J. Lowe
and M. L. Dockrill

Routledge & Kegan Paul

London and Boston

First published 1972
by Routledge and Kegan Paul Ltd
Broadway House, 68–74 Carter Lane,
London, EC4V 5EL
and 9 Park Street,
Boston, Mass. 02108, U.S.A.
Printed in Great Britain by
Western Printing Services Ltd, Bristol
© *C. J. Lowe and M. L. Dockrill 1972*
ISBN 0 7100 7092 6

Great God, I often think that the world of international diplomacy is the dirtiest thing alive and that a Statesman is a synonym for a knave.

Curzon, 1922

Contents

Volume I

Contents

Volume II

Contents

Volume III

Preface

While this work endeavours to continue the policy of the first volume in this series, i.e. to utilize recent specialist studies in order to produce a book of manageable length for students, the bulk of this volume is necessarily based on original research by both authors in numerous archives and private papers. Although there is a steady trickle of monographs in this period, large areas were still untouched at the time of writing. Nevertheless, in an attempt at brevity, only the major aspects of policy have been discussed, which has led to many omissions, of which the authors are fully conscious.

We should like first to acknowledge the gracious permission of Her Majesty the Queen to quote material from the Royal Archives at Windsor Castle.

We are also grateful to the Controller of Her Majesty's Stationery Office for permission to quote from unpublished Crown Copyright material in the Public Record Office, to the Trustees of the British Museum for permission to reproduce material in the Balfour and J. A. Spender papers in the Department of Western Manuscripts, to the Secretary of State for Foreign and Commonwealth Affairs for permission to transcribe unpublished Crown Copyright material in the India Office Library and to the Trustees of the National Library of Scotland for permission to quote from the Haldane Papers. Others who kindly gave us permission to quote from unpublished material of which they own the copyright are: the Trustees of the Beaverbrook Library and Beaverbrook Newspapers (Lloyd George papers), Mr Mark Bonham Carter (Asquith papers), Lord Harcourt, the Clerk of the Records of the House of Lords Records Office (Samuel Papers), and Mr Laurence P. Scott (C. P. Scott papers).

We should like to thank Mr Robert Mackworth-Young and the staff at Windsor Castle, Mr A. J. P. Taylor and the staff of the Beaverbrook Library, Lord Harcourt, and the Librarians at all the

Preface

Archives listed above for their helpful and patient assistance during the time we were engaged on these researches. We are grateful to the editors of the *Historical Journal* and the *Canadian Journal of History* for permission to reprint material in Vol. II, Ch. 1 which first appeared in these periodicals. Our thanks are due, also, to the Canada Council for their generous aid in the summer of 1969, which greatly assisted the rapid conclusion of this work, and to Portsmouth Polytechnic.

Finally, we should like to express our gratitude to Professor W. N. Medlicott, for the advice and encouragement he has given to the authors both during his tenure of the Stevenson Chair of International History in the University of London and in his retirement.

C. J. LOWE
M. L. DOCKRILL

AUTHORS' NOTE

It was not thought necessary always to identify the various (Departmental) Offices held by Ministers, especially after the beginning of the First World War, when the game of musical chairs really began in earnest, when new Departments were created, and later dissolved, with increasing frequency, and when Ministers came and went with great rapidity. The interested reader is advised to consult the useful lists of Cabinet Ministers and their posts contained in the appendices of Sir Robert Ensor's *England, 1870–1914* (Oxford, 1936) and A. J. P. Taylor's *English History 1914–1945* (Oxford, 1965).

C.J.L.
M.L.D.

Abbreviations

B.D.	British Documents on the Origins of the War, 1898–1914
Cab.	Cabinet Papers
C.I.D.	Committee of Imperial Defence
EUR.D.	Morley Papers (India Office)
F.O.	Foreign Office Correspondence
Geo.V.	Royal Archives (post-1910)
V.I.C.	Royal Archives (pre-1910)

Chapter 1

The Anglo-French Entente

> A better understanding with France would not improb-
> ably be the precursor of a better understanding with
> Russia.
>
> *Lansdowne*, 1903

Introduction

The Anglo-Japanese alliance and the end of the Boer War on 31
May 1902 enabled Lansdowne to face the future with greater confidence, and temporarily lessened the urgency for a settlement of
outstanding problems with France and Russia. This was evident
from his response when, in August 1902, Paul Cambon, the
French Ambassador in London, put out feelers for an Anglo-
French agreement on Morocco and Siam. Lansdowne, fearing
complications with Germany and Austria, decided to await a more
favourable moment. Although he recognized that the political
and economic influence of France in Morocco was increasing, he
hoped that the country could be kept going as a nominally independent state, at least for a few more years.[1]

Nevertheless, it was still evident that in the long run an accommodation with these two powers would be of advantage. Britain's
commitments were still as over-extended as against her resources
as they had been in the 1890s,[2] whilst in addition England now
wanted to avoid all conflicts with these Powers so that she could
concentrate on recovering from the stresses and strains imposed
by the long, drawn-out South African struggle. The Committee of
Imperial Defence, the Elgin Committee (to enquire into the
disasters in South Africa) and the Esher Committee on War Office
reform were all established by Balfour in 1902–3.[3]

Of the two it was France's ally, Russia, who represented the
more dangerous threat to British security, especially in India,
and with her the atmosphere for negotiations appeared to be
more propitious in the months following the signature of the

1

Anglo-Japanese alliance. The alliance relieved the Admiralty from some of its more pressing problems in Far Eastern waters,[4] and British satisfaction with developments in that theatre was further increased when, in April 1902, Russia agreed to withdraw her troops from Manchuria in stages over a period of eighteen months, commencing in October 1902. The way now seemed clear for a Russo-Japanese settlement. Japan was still anxious to discuss with Russia their future relations in Manchuria and Korea, the British had no really vital interests in these areas and, provided that the Anglo-Japanese alliance was not affected by any Russo-Japanese agreement, Lansdowne was not alarmed by the prospect: indeed he was relieved that the alliance had not encouraged Japanese intransigence.[5]

A satisfactory Russo-Japanese arrangement might react favourably on Anglo-Russian relations. The British seemed helpless both militarily and economically to resist Russia's penetration of the countries bordering India. Persia was the most serious problem, although rumours of Russian intrigues in Afghanistan and Tibet were also causing considerable perturbation in Calcutta and in London. The Government of India feared that Persia would eventually succumb entirely to Russia's influence. Even if the Russians occupied the north of the country, England doubted that her financial and military resources were adequate to enable her to make an equivalent advance in the south.[6] An arrangement with Russia about these areas seemed the obvious solution, but although Lansdowne made several approaches to Russia during 1902 and 1903, and had friendly exchanges with the new Russian Ambassador, Count Benckendorff, Russia's response was scarcely encouraging.

Relations with Germany were also causing Lansdowne increasing concern. During the summer of 1902 there was a serious quarrel between the two countries over concessions in the Yangtze valley. German press and Reichstag attacks on the conduct of the British Army in South Africa naturally aroused great resentment in Great Britain and provoked angry ripostes. Lansdowne was greatly alarmed by the rising anti-German tide in England which was affecting the Cabinet, the Foreign Office and the Admiralty, as well as public opinion.[7] Apart from China and the Baghdad Railway there appeared to be few tangible grounds for poor relations between the two countries. The Admiralty, it was true, was concerned about the growth and efficiency of the German navy, but its fears were only just beginning to affect public opinion to any great degree. Lansdowne hoped that the ill-feeling would soon subside; as early as 22 April 1902 he wrote to the British Ambassador at Berlin, Sir Frank Lascelles, that, 'I am sanguine enough to hope that the bitter feeling which now prevails against us in Germany may not last for ever.'[8]

Lansdowne's efforts to ameliorate relations by co-operating with Germany to solve two questions which affected the interests of both countries—Venezuela and the Baghdad Railway—merely exacerbated the existing ill-feeling. In December 1902 British and German warships blockaded Venezuela, whose failure to pay her debts to foreign creditors had long exasperated the British and German Governments. However, the affair assumed a rather different aspect when the German commander bombarded the Venezuelan port of Maracaibo in January 1903. Opinion in the United States, already uneasy about the Anglo-German venture, was outraged, and suspicions were voiced that Germany had more ambitious designs than the collection of her debts from Venezuela. The British press soon took up the cry, and alarmist reports were published that England might become involved in a war with the United States for the sake of Germany's ambitions in Central America. The uproar came at a difficult moment for Lansdowne, since he was edging towards a settlement of the Alaskan boundary dispute with the United States.[9] Venezuela's debt problems were eventually settled by recourse to arbitration, but Lansdowne was irritated by the fuss, especially as the Germans 'ran straight as far as we were concerned'.[10]

The prospect of a settlement of the Baghdad Railway question became more hopeful during 1902. Before 1900 the British had viewed with relative indifference the potential threat to their economic and strategic interests in Turkey and the Persian Gulf posed by this railway. The Sultan had granted a concession to an Anglo-German combine in 1888 to build a railway from Constantinople to Angora in Anatolia. In 1892 he granted a further concession to the Company to extend the line to Konia. The Anatolian Railway Company was by now solely German owned, the British financiers having sold their interests to their partners in 1890. In January 1902 the Company secured Turkish authority to extend the line via Adana and Mosul to Baghdad, its ultimate destination being Basra and the Gulf, where Company agents had been active in 1900 in searching for a suitable terminus. The Company, however, now required Anglo-French capital if it were to make further progress in constructing the line, and in 1902 it approached British financiers with a view to obtaining British investment in the enterprise. Lansdowne, keenly aware of the importance of the railway, was eager to secure British participation, and was even prepared to recommend the injection of British Government funds if British capitalists did not come forward. In return he wanted to secure the internationalization of the railway as far as Baghdad, plus British control of any branch built from Baghdad to the Gulf. In his view England could not expect to delay the completion of the line indefinitely, and since it would encourage the expansion of trade in the Middle East, from which British traders would profit, he thought that a reasonable settlement would be of benefit to all parties, as well as conducing to better Anglo-German relations. He therefore encouraged the British bankers to negotiate an agreement with their German counterparts.[11]

British public opinion, however, did not share his enthusiasm, and there was an outcry in the press and Parliament when it became known, in 1903, that the Government was contemplating this further measure of co-operation with Germany. Eventually, in April 1903, after attacks on his proposals in the Cabinet, led by the now anti-German Joseph Chamberlain, Lansdowne was compelled to abandon an agreement which had been drawn up so laboriously by the Anglo-German financiers, and which provided for Franco-British participation in the line. 'I am afraid that in the long run our attitude will be hard to explain,' Lansdowne lamented. The Government could only fall back on warnings as a means of defending British interests in the Gulf—in May 1903 Lansdowne told the House of Lords that England would 'regard the establishment of a naval base or of a fortified port in the Persian Gulf as a very grave menace to our interests'. There the question rested for the time being.[12]

The Negotiation of the Entente

During 1903 Lansdowne became more anxious to reach agreement with France, a result of the deteriorating situation in the Far

East, and of the outbreak of serious unrest in Morocco at the
end of 1902, which, he feared, would lead to international complications unless France and England reached agreement on the
future of the country.[13] His efforts were encouraged by Joseph
Chamberlain, who was now a fervent advocate of an entente with
France, and had become extremely suspicious of Germany. 'She
is more unpopular than France ever was,' he wrote in October
1903.[14]

In the Far East the triumph of the forward party in the councils of
the Tsar was demonstrated by the refusal of the Russian Government to complete the withdrawal of her troops from Manchuria,
and by increasing Russian activity on the borders of Korea. The
Foreign Secretary reasoned that a friendly France would restrain
Russia from impetuous action in the Far East which might precipitate a war with Japan. Should the worst happen and hostilities
break out between Japan and Russia, a neutral France might
enable England to escape involvement in the struggle. France too
had no wish to become embroiled in the Far Eastern adventures of
her ally, while Delcassé, long suspicious of Germany's ambitions, was keen to settle the Moroccan question with England.
Relations between the two countries were much improved as a
result of King Edward's successful visit to Paris in May 1903 and
a return visit to London by President Loubet in July, which
enabled Lansdowne to enter into direct negotiations with Delcassé, who accompanied the President. On 7 July the two men
discussed the framework of a possible settlement, which was to
include British recognition of France's preponderant position in
Morocco, in return for French recognition of the British position
in Egypt, the protection of Britain's strategic interest in Tangier
and agreements on Newfoundland, Siam and the New Hebrides.

The advantages of a Franco-British agreement became even
more obvious during the summer and autumn as relations between
England and Russia and between Japan and Russia continued to
deteriorate. To the crisis in the Far East was added renewed tension in the Near East in the spring, when a serious revolt against
the Turks broke out in Macedonia.[15] For a time Lansdowne
feared that Bulgaria would intervene on behalf of the Macedonians, with the prospect of England and Russia being drawn in

on opposite sides in the ensuing Turco-Bulgarian war. The immediate crisis died down in the autumn when Russia and Austria-Hungary drew up a new reform scheme for the province, which proved to be as futile as previous efforts by the two Powers to ease the lot of the inhabitants.[16] King Edward might grumble at the feeble British response to the situation in Macedonia, but Lansdowne recognized that England, isolated at Constantinople,[17] had little chance of persuading the Porte to accept reforms, and that even limited action by Austria and Russia was better than no action at all. One hopeful sign was that Lansdowne had managed to get negotiations started with Russia on Central Asia, although they had little chance of success while Japan and Russia were steadily drifting towards war.

Discussions between Japan and Russia on the Far East continued during the autumn and winter of 1903, but as a result of Russian obstructiveness they made little progress. Russia was behaving more and more arrogantly in Manchuria, and was stepping up her efforts to penetrate Korea. Thus, by the end of 1903, the British were faced for the first time with the prospect of a conflict between Japan and Russia. As a result the alliance with Japan was now regarded in London as a serious liability, since it was not thought that the Japanese army and navy stood much chance against the Russian colossus. Although the Treasury warned the Cabinet that British finances could not stand the strain of war, few Ministers believed that Britain could stand aside while Japan was being crushed—it would be a terrible blow to British prestige as well as to her own interests. Thus, even if France remained neutral, England might still have to intervene in the conflict. Lansdowne and his colleagues hoped, however, that Japan would at least be able to hold her islands against Russia. The King summed up the position on 1 January 1904:

> It looked to him that if France should join Russia in the coming conflict then we should be bound to take part with Japan. But if France stood out, the King agreed with the Prime Minister, it was only in the improbable contingency that Russia would crush Japan that any question of England's intervention would arise.[18]

It was a gloomy outlook. Russia's victory would confirm her hegemony in the Far East, would make her more difficult to deal with elsewhere, and would lead to the absorption of Japan into

6

Russia's sphere of influence. In consequence British naval and military estimates would have to be dramatically increased. On the other hand, British statesmen shrank from the equally dangerous course of intervention in a war over Manchuria and Korea, areas in which British interests were negligible, with Russia extending the conflict into Central Asia, with France as a belligerent, and with Germany, if she did not come in on Russia's side, using the occasion to extract concessions from Great Britain as the price for her neutrality.[19] As Balfour commented in January 1904, 'I trust that whatever the course of events in the Far East, this country will not be dragged into hostilities, as for obvious reasons this could hardly occur without involving half, or more than half, the world, in a war which would benefit nobody but the neutrals and chiefly Germany,'[20] while the anti-German Louis Mallet of the Foreign Office warned the Prime Minister that 'Germany will leave no stone unturned to involve us in the war, and if she succeeded we should be at her mercy'.[21]

Lansdowne was extremely pessimistic. By the end of December 1903, he was even prepared to throw Japan overboard by informing her that she should accept any reasonable Russian offer concerning Korea. He dwelt on the risks at stake if war broke out. British public opinion might insist on England coming to the aid of her ally if the latter were in danger of being crushed, a course which would aggravate England's already pressing financial difficulties. 'For these reasons I should like H.M. Govt. to try its hand as a mediator or at all events as a friendly counsellor, rather than wait until it can appear on the scene as a "deliverer",' he wrote.[22] However, he was overruled by Balfour and the other Ministers, who insisted that England must maintain the alliance, and not alienate Japan by offering her unwelcome advice, or by proposing mediation.[23] On the other hand the British Government was anxious to avoid upsetting Russia too much, since it still hoped, eventually, to resume the Central Asian negotiations with her. Lansdowne assured Benckendorff on 8 February that England intended to remain neutral, and Austen Chamberlain, the chancellor, supported by Balfour (who thought it might be regarded as 'an act of war'), refused to provide a loan to the Japanese, who had to depend on private British sources during the war.[24]

The outbreak of war between Russia and Japan on 8 February

1904 encouraged the British and French to hasten the conclusion
of their negotiations, which had begun in earnest the previous
September. Nevertheless there were last-minute delays. Delcassé
was anxious to secure the Gambia in return for the loss of French
fishing rights in Newfoundland, a demand which was rejected by
Lansdowne and the Cabinet as excessive. Eventually, in February, Lansdowne agreed to the transfer of the West African Iles
de Los to France. When France rejected this offer as inadequate,
the Foreign Secretary threatened to break off the negotiations.
Although France gave way, she did not give up hope of securing
the Gambia in the years down to 1914.

The agreement was signed on 8 April 1904. It was a compre-
hensive, although by no means a final, settlement of Anglo-
French differences in the colonial field. It consisted of two con-
ventions, the first dealing with Newfoundland and West and
Central Africa, and the second with Siam, Madagascar and the
New Hebrides. Finally there was a declaration about Morocco,
and five secret articles. France abandoned her pressure for
England's withdrawal from Egypt and pledged her support for
changes in the Egyptian financial régime. In return for this
belated recognition of British predominance in Egypt, England
recognized the right of France to preserve order in Morocco, and
to assist the Sultan in reforming his administration and economy.
The open door was to be maintained in both Egypt and Morocco
for thirty years. France promised to reach agreement with Spain
respecting Spanish interests in Morocco, and agreed not to erect
fortifications on the Moorish coast opposite Gibraltar. The secret
articles alluded to the possibility of the modification of the status
quo by the two countries in Egypt and Morocco, assigned the
Melilla coast to Spain in that event, and referred to the possibility
of the abolition of the capitulations in Egypt and Morocco.

Lord Cromer had done much to smooth the way towards
agreement, urging on Lansdowne concessions where compromise
was indicated, and he even renamed Fashoda to please the French.
He wrote to Balfour in October 1903 that:

> To my mind the two greatest dangers at present are backwardness in
> education and unsound finance—by which term I mean more
> specifically spending more money than we can afford. I cannot help
> indulging in a hope that the French negotiation, if brought to a
> successful termination, may open the way to a better order of things

8

without in any way endangering all that is essential in the policy of modern Imperialism.[25]

It was at Cromer's behest that France was induced to agree to a clause whereby each party was pledged to support the other diplomatically to secure the execution of the declarations on Morocco and Egypt—Cromer suspected that Germany would make difficulties in Egypt. While Cromer believed that the convention was worth more to England than to France—after all Britain was already in possession of Egypt—there is little doubt that this clause was of greater value to France in the succeeding years than it ever was to Britain, as Lansdowne had not foreseen its European implications.[26]

The Entente reduced the likelihood of a war between France and Britain in the Far East; since, however, both countries were determined to remain neutral in any case, the convention merely registered their decision. In its own right, of course, the agreement was a sensible settlement of the colonial questions which had divided them for so long. For his part Lansdowne hoped that it would lead in the future to the long anticipated settlement with Russia, in which France would act as mediator. Thus, despite the war in the Far East, Lansdowne was far from abandoning his hopes for an eventual *rapprochement* with Russia. Sir Charles Hardinge, an enthusiast for an Anglo-Russian agreement, was appointed Ambassador to St Petersburg in May 1904, and soon after his arrival he persuaded the Tsar to agree in principle to a future settlement. Thanks to Hardinge's efforts the inevitable tensions which arose between the two countries did not leave behind them a permanent legacy of bitterness on either side. The worst incident, of course, was the Dogger Bank affair (on the night of 21/22 October 1904) when the ramshackle Russian Baltic Fleet, which was on its way to the Pacific, shot up some British fishing vessels in mistake for Japanese warships. Public and official opinion in England was greatly inflamed against Russia and Lansdowne's hand was nearly forced. Fortunately in the nick of time Russia announced her regrets and agreed that the Hague court should assess the damages. 'The hot heads who want us to bluster and bounce' had nearly involved England in a futile war; fortunately other incidents were not nearly so serious.[27]

Japan's military and naval victories came as a welcome surprise to her British ally, who had contributed little in material terms to Japan's success, and who had originally anticipated, as the very least that could be hoped for, a stalemate in the Far East followed by a compromise settlement. By her defeat of the Baltic Fleet on 28 May 1905, Japan reduced the Russian navy to a negligible quantity, and at last justified the alliance in the eyes of the British. Japan's friendship was now worth having and Lansdowne even refused to support President Roosevelt's efforts during the summer of 1905 to persuade Tokyo to accept a reasonable peace settlement.[28] The Foreign Secretary had no intention of upsetting Japan by pressing unpalatable advice upon her, even if his refusal occasioned Roosevelt temporary irritation.[29] By May the British Government resolved to renew the Japanese alliance, and, at the same time, to extend its terms.

The Cabinet reasoned that the now powerful Japan might be able to solve some of Britain's more pressing difficulties on the borders of India. The Committee of Imperial Defence (C.I.D.) feared that Russia, baulked in the Far East, might embark on an all-out effort to bring Afghanistan, Tibet and Persia under her sway. While the Government of India was pressing for large increases in its military establishment to meet this contingency, the War Office confessed that it had insufficient troops available. In any case the Government had no wish to increase its military expenditure; the Chancellor of the Exchequer, Austen Chamberlain, wrote in April 1904, that, 'however reluctant we may be to face the fact, the time had come when we must frankly admit that the financial resources of the U.K. are inadequate to do all that we should desire in the matter of Imperial Defence'.[30] Since an Anglo-Russian agreement was obviously out of the question for the time being, the British thought that, as an alternative, they might be able to persuade Tokyo to send Japanese troops to India, if necessary, to help repel a Russian advance. Thus Britain's Central Asian policy was refurbished in 1905. The British obligation to defend Afghanistan was reaffirmed, after some hesitation, by the Amir, and the Japanese were persuaded to accept an additional clause in the alliance which authorized the despatch of Japanese troops to India should hostilities break out there between Russia and England. For her part England agreed to support Japan's policy in Korea, and to make the alliance operative in the event of either party being attacked by a third Power.[31]

The revised alliance was signed on 12 August 1905. For all its novel features it had little relevance to British policy down to 1914. In 1906 the Committee of Imperial Defence decided against using Japanese troops in India. In the event of war with Russia the Japanese army would be better employed in Manchuria; besides there was the factor of British prestige in India to consider. Furthermore, the danger of a renewed outbreak of war in the Far East receded after 1906 as Japan and Russia, and England and Russia settled their differences. Sir Edward Grey, Lansdowne's successor, concentrated his attention on Europe, and while upholding the Anglo-Japanese alliance, took little interest in it. Of course it remained important in that the Japanese navy continued to protect British interests in the Far East, while in defiance of her promises, England further reduced the number of her warships in that theatre.

The First Moroccan Crisis

The Russo-Japanese war had thus resulted in unexpectedly welcome benefits for British policy makers, who could, after May 1905, face the future with a new air of confidence. Nevertheless, they had had several shocks during the hostilities, not least being the possibility of a conjunction between Germany and Russia. The Germans had approached St Petersburg several times towards the end of 1904 hinting at a possible Russo-German alliance, and in July 1905 William II actually persuaded the Russian emperor, at their Björkö meeting, to sign a treaty. Nothing came of these intrigues since Russia could not afford to alienate France, whose capital they required to restore the shattered Russian economy. But the risk seemed a real one to the British at the time. and it encouraged Lansdowne to expedite the renewal of the Japanese alliance, as well as to revive, temporarily at least, his desire for a settlement with Russia.

These German activities increased British suspicions of her restless policy. Relations between the two countries continued to deteriorate during 1904 and 1905. King Edward and his German nephew were on the worst of terms, and even Lansdowne, after reading accounts of what the German Emperor had said to the Tsar at Björkö, exclaimed, 'I must say that the description of the Kaiser's language and demeanour fills me with disquiet. What may not a man in such a frame of mind do next.'[32]

His anxiety in this respect had already been aroused by the Emperor's flamboyant descent on Tangier on 31 March 1905, and by his dramatic pledge to uphold the independence of the Sultan's dominions.[33] Bülow's intention, in promoting this venture, was not only to affirm Germany's interests in Morocco, but to force the French to recognize that co-operation with Germany, and not England, was the best course for France. Germany's grievances about developments in Morocco were not entirely unjustified. Delcassé had made no effort to associate Germany in the network of agreements he had made with England, Italy and Spain concerning Morocco, and he had in fact tried to mislead the *Wilhelmstrasse* as to the true motives behind the Anglo-French convention. By 1905 the French, fortified by their agreements, had begun to assert their predominance in the country, and early in the year they despatched a French mission to Fez to persuade the Sultan to introduce a programme of reforms under French supervision. This was regarded by Germany as a prelude to a French take-over of Morocco.[34] Germany might have expected that England, with her substantial trading interests in Morocco, would support her in upholding the independence of the country. By 1905, of course, this was impossible. England was bound to support France by her convention; moreover persistent German unfriendliness in the preceding years had taken its toll of British goodwill. Lansdowne had been irritated by the difficulties Germany had made about changes in the financial régime in Egypt in 1904, and by her efforts to align Russia in an anti-British combination. The Kaiser's Tangier initiative convinced many of Lansdowne's officials that Germany had embarked on a determined effort to wreck the Anglo-French Entente.

Hence Lansdowne was determined to support Delcassé, particularly as the latter was opposed in the French Cabinet by a group led by Rouvier, the Prime Minister. Rouvier wanted to reach agreement with Germany on Morocco, by offering Germany a Moroccan port in return for her recognition of France's paramount position in the country. Here British interests were directly involved since Lansdowne believed that a German port on Morocco's Atlantic, or even worse, Mediterranean coast, would be fatal to British security. First Lansdowne agreed to support, on treaty grounds, the French demand for the introduction by the Sultan of a series of reforms under French surveillance.

These reforms included the placing of the police at the Moorish ports under the control of French officers. Germany countered by proposing, on 8 April, an international conference to discuss the Moroccan question. Germany was confident that most of the Great Powers would support her demand for the reforms and police to be placed under international control. On 11 April, however, Lansdowne joined France in rejecting the German proposal. By this time Rouvier and his colleagues, encouraged by German hints, were plainly anxious to get rid of Delcassé, confident that his departure would facilitate the deal with Germany on which they were intent.

Lansdowne and Balfour fully appreciated that the disappearance of the French Foreign Minister, fêted as the architect of the Entente, would be represented as a severe blow to British prestige and, even worse, would open the way to a Franco-German agreement affecting British strategic interests. Lansdowne therefore promised, on 23 April, to support France in resisting a German demand for a Moroccan port, although he would make no promise of British assistance should the Moroccan question lead to a Franco-German war. The British Ambassador to France, Sir Francis Bertie, realized that Lansdowne's offer was inadequate to save Delcassè, and both he and Louis Mallet urged their superior that unless he came forward with more concrete pledges to France, Rouvier would triumph.[35] Lansdowne, however, firmly resisted this advice. He had no intention of promising British military and naval aid to France—indeed the British gave little consideration, at this stage in the crisis, as to how they would react, beyond protesting, if Germany should secure a Moroccan port.

However, German pressure on France became more intense during May, and Delcassé's position became still more difficult. Lansdowne informed the French ambassador, Paul Cambon, on 17 May that:

> Our two governments should continue to treat one another with the most absolute confidence, should keep one another fully informed of everything which came to their knowledge, and should, as far as possible, discuss in advance any contingencies by which they might in the course of events find themselves confronted.[36]

Cambon and Delcassé believed that Lansdowne had virtually

offered an alliance against Germany, or, at least, had agreed that
Britain would support France in the event of a Franco-German
war. Indeed this misapprehension could only be reinforced by
unofficial hints to this effect by Bertie, and by the indiscretions of
British service chiefs in conversation with their French counterparts, when they insinuated that England would not leave France
in the lurch. The wording of his statement, together with that of
an explanatory note to the French on 25 May, made it clear that
Lansdowne only intended to ensure that France did not enter
into an agreement with Germany affecting British interests, without first giving the British an opportunity to have their say. Lansdowne, although irritated by her methods of diplomacy, did not
believe that Germany intended to attack France, although he too
recognized that in the last resort England would have to come to
the assistance of France if Germany attacked her.[37]

Delcassé's manoeuvre failed. Rouvier, who also believed that
England would enter into an alliance with France, did not think
that British military assistance would be of much use. Fearing a
war with Germany, in which a weakened Russia would be unable
to support her ally, he secured Delcassé's resignation on 6 June
1904. While this was greeted with much anguish in London as a
blow to the Entente, it did not have any serious, long run consequence as far as the British were concerned. In the short run it
destroyed Lansdowne's confidence, such as it was, in France's
will and determination—he tended to blame French weakness
rather than German bullying for the outcome. Balfour wrote to
the King on 8 June that:

> Delcassé's dismissal or resignation under pressure from the German
> Government displayed a weakness on the part of France which
> indicated that she could not at present be counted as an effective
> force in international politics. She could no longer be trusted not to
> yield to threats at the critical moment of a negotiation.[38]

Nevertheless, the British did not view Delcassé's departure too
tragically. As a result of Japan's naval victory over Russia at
Tsushima a serious rival had been destroyed and England's world
position was in consequence a strong one. Furthermore Rouvier
was unable to secure the coveted agreement with Germany and,
in the face of the latter's bullying and uncompromising tactics, he
was soon forced to adopt Delcassé's policy. Germany, made over-

confident by her recent success, and saddled with her open commitment to a conference, rejected Rouvier's approach for bilateral talks on Morocco, and France once again had to look to Lansdowne for diplomatic assistance. The Foreign Secretary, himself alarmed by increasing German belligerence, told the German Ambassador, Count Metternich, on 28 June, that if Germany attacked France, he doubted that British public opinion would allow the Government to remain neutral. Nevertheless, as he informed the Ambassador, he did not contemplate an alliance with France; indeed he did not even tell the French about his initiative. Thereafter the Moroccan crisis receded as a dangerous issue during the short time left to the Unionists. Germany became more conciliatory towards the French in the late summer in the vain hope that France might adhere to the Björkö treaty, and eventually the two countries reached agreement on the holding of a conference at Algeciras in January 1906, at which French interests in the policing of the frontier with Algeria would be safeguarded.³⁹

With the conclusion of the Treaty of Portsmouth between Russia and Japan on 5 September 1905, Lansdowne's patient and cautious diplomacy during the war received its justification. British confidence was such that even an agreement with Russia no longer seemed quite so pressing—Russia, it was thought, would take years to recover from her humiliation. Nevertheless, there were increasing signs that British foreign policy might soon change its direction; that Europe rather than the Empire might become the focus of attention. Already towards the end of 1905 the War Office and the Admiralty were contemplating the possibility of providing naval and military assistance to France in the event of a Franco-German war. With the disappearance of the Russian threat overseas, that of Germany in Europe was becoming more prominent. Although Lansdowne tended to regard these military plans merely as academic speculations, his successor was to take them much more seriously.

Grey, Algeciras and the Strengthening of the Entente

By the winter the Unionists' Parliamentary and internal difficulties had become so intense that on 4 December 1905 Balfour resigned, and seven days later Sir Henry Campbell-Bannerman managed to form a Government composed of an uneasy coalition of former Liberal Imperialists and pro-Boers. After some hesitation Sir Edward Grey accepted the post of Foreign Secretary and, with his advent, British foreign policy underwent a distinct change of emphasis. The general election of January 1906, which resulted in a massive Liberal majority, appeared to confirm the desire of the electorate for an unadventurous policy abroad. Tariff reform, which Joseph Chamberlain envisaged as a means of uniting the Empire, was decisively rejected; Britain was to continue on the proven path of free trade. The Liberals were for the most part opposed to further additions to the burdens of Empire; and although few of them evinced any desire to give any part of the existing structure away, many hoped that reforms would be introduced, particularly in India and South Africa, and believed that British imperialism should work for the benefit of its colonial subjects.[40]

Grey accepted this verdict on the election. His policy abroad was genuinely pacific and non-provocative. The new Foreign Secretary was born in London in 1862, the son of the owner of a small estate in Northumberland. His family had a distinguished record of public service—Grey was related to the Earl Grey of the Reform Bill, and his grandfather, Sir George Grey, had served as Home Secretary in the middle years of the nineteenth century. Grey himself entered Parliament as a Liberal Member for his home constituency of the Berwick-on-Tweed division of Northumberland, after a fairly undistinguished academic record at Winchester and Balliol. He served as Parliamentary Under-Secretary for Foreign Affairs under Rosebery and Kimberley between 1892 and 1895, and even in opposition his work was mostly confined to foreign affairs. He sided with his close friends Asquith and Haldane under Rosebery's banner against the pro-Boers in the great Liberal schism from 1899 to 1902—this may have accounted for much of the subsequent Liberal distrust of his foreign policy. The free trade issue virtually reunited the party, and the growing split after 1903 in the ranks of the Unionists put fresh heart into Liberals up and down the country.[41]

Grey was subjected to more violent attacks on his foreign policy, both from contemporaries and later writers, than perhaps were endured by any of his predecessors in that office. His critics accused him of excessive secretiveness in the operation of his policy, particularly in his dealings with the Cabinet, with the intention of pursuing a policy of his own design in Europe, a policy which, by so strengthening Britain's diplomatic and military ties with France, led eventually and inevitably to England's involvement in the first world war. He has been described as aloof, reserved, reticent, upright and honest, yet lacking in resourcefulness and enterprise.[42] Many commented adversely on his insularity, his reluctance to go abroad and his preference for English and Scottish country life.[43] Others complained that his moralist approach to public affairs led to a certain inflexibility in the operation of his foreign policy.

Inevitably there is a grain of truth, and yet not the whole truth, in some of these observations. Grey was indeed a cautious Foreign Secretary, disinclined, like Salisbury and Lansdowne, to take risks, and highly conscious of the element of continuity in British foreign policy. However, as has already been suggested, his caution reflected the unwillingness of British public opinion to contemplate an adventurous foreign policy; it was also perhaps, an advantage, given the disturbed state of Europe between 1906 and 1914. His chief critics were often disillusioned Liberals—as J. L. Hammond put it later, 'seldom indeed has a Government or Minister encountered such severe criticism from political opponents as Grey encountered from his political friends'.[44] Grey himself referred in 1908 to

> those whose emotions are stronger than their heads, who overestimate by 100% the amount of good which the British Government can do to the human race and don't estimate at all the complications into which we might get by following their advice.[45]

One example of his difficulty in this respect is provided by E. D. Morel, whose Congo Reform Association did so much in these years to publicize the cruelties of King Leopold's régime in the Congo. By 1913 Grey had succeeded in achieving an equitable settlement of the Congo question; but the necessarily slow pace of the negotiations with Belgium soon lost Grey the sympathy of the impatient Morel, who proceeded to embark on public attacks on Grey's entire European policy.[46] Nor was there any truth in the assertion that Grey neglected his duties by frequent absences from London. He was never free from the demands of Office, despatch boxes followed him wherever he went, and he was seldom out of touch with the Foreign Office.[47] He also took a leading, if self-effacing, part in all the major domestic crises of the day, and, unlike his predecessors, was forced to attend at the same time to the rigorous business of the House of Commons.

Grey had worked out a rationale for his foreign policy, unlike Lansdowne, who often seemed to react empirically to the exigencies of the moment. Lansdowne, as befitted a former Viceroy of India, had concentrated on the effects of his policy on the Empire while Grey, on the other hand, was more concerned with Europe. Lansdowne's alliance with Japan, and the Entente with France became, for Grey, the means by which Britain could contain what he regarded as an ambitious and restless Germany. His policy was certainly dominated by his experiences as Under-Secretary in the 1890s, when it seemed to him that Germany had used England's difficulties with France and Russia to extract concessions as a price for her support for British policy in Egypt and elsewhere. He shared the assumption of many of his contemporaries that Germany had become a danger to British security in Europe, and that consequently the policy of isolation had become a serious liability to British interests. Thus in the 1920s he could still write that 'German policy seems to have been based upon a deliberate belief that moral scruples and altruistic motives do not count in international affairs . . . The highest morality for a German Government was the national interest.'[48] True his approach tended at times to make his policy rather rigid. A certain double-standard crept in whereby Austro-German failings were severely condemned, while those of Russia and France were often, but not always, minimized. But this tendency has been exaggerated for, as will be shown, Grey became more flexible after 1911. But given Grey's belief that German policy was peculiarly malevolent—'the making of mischief between other Powers and the poisoning of one mind against the other'[49]—there could be little real friendship between the two countries, despite his frequent expressions of his desire for better relations with her.

His advent to office coincided with changes in the composition and organization of the Foreign Office which, for the first time, gave his officials a role in the formulation of foreign policy.[50] Clerks were at last becoming specialists, and this less amateur approach to the work was also evident in other areas of the public administration (except in the Cabinet). At the same time younger men were moving into the higher echelons of the foreign service. These officials were convinced that Germany was England's most dangerous enemy on the continent, and they insisted that only by means of close understandings with France and Russia could England resist Germany's ambitions, which they conceived to be on a Napoleonic scale. Reforms in the office filing system enabled even the most junior officials to express their opinions on policy matters by means of minutes or comments on the white foolscap sheets which now encased every incoming telegram and despatch. Advice of this sort would never have been tolerated by Lord Salisbury, but Lansdowne had accepted that some changes were necessary in order to give his staff more stimulating and responsible work than the routine, soul destroying work that they had been employed on hitherto. The reforms, in which Eyre Crowe and Sir Charles Hardinge were closely involved, were intended to reduce the amount of paper going to the Foreign Secretary by filtering all the incoming correspondence so that he only saw the more important material. In practice, however, with the ever-increasing work handled by the Foreign Office after 1906, and the new minuting system, which created a vast amount of additional reading, these reforms failed in their ultimate intention. As a result, Grey was always grossly overworked.[51]

Nevertheless, the reforms enabled the anti-Germans to express their views on foreign policy, often at inordinate length. By 1906 their influence in the Office predominated. Lansdowne had been reluctant to promote the more extreme Germanophobes, but their ability was undeniable. Furthermore they received the powerful backing of King Edward, whose somewhat changeable views on policy might often be ignored, but whose influence on foreign service appointments was still decisive. The King and Sir Charles Hardinge were close friends, a factor which was obviously of crucial importance to the anti-German clique, who looked to Hardinge as their mentor. In 1904 Hardinge secured the appointment of the able Sir Francis Bertie, who had himself assisted Hardinge's promotion earlier, as Ambassador to Paris, the most influential post in the service. Other officials who were imbued with distrust of Germany—Eyre Crowe, William Tyrrell (eventually Grey's secretary), and Louis Mallet, among others—all secured preferment at this time and eventually rose to high positions in the service. This process culminated in Hardinge's promotion in January 1906 to the post of Permanent Under-Secretary. Not only was his competence unquestionable, but both Lansdowne and the King hoped that he would act as a brake on the introduction of startling innovations in foreign policy by the Liberals. His place at St Petersburg was taken in 1906 by Sir Arthur Nicolson, who became a fanatical adherent of the Anglo-Russian Entente as a bulwark against Germany.

Faced, on his appointment, with an Office that was steadily becoming dominated by the anti-Germans, Grey, relatively inexperienced, was bound, to some extent, to be influenced by their advice. The chief exponent of the anti-German line was the extremely hard-working and able Eyre Crowe, the senior clerk in the Western Department. In minute after minute Crowe ventilated his thesis that Germany was bent on seizing European and world hegemony and that only Britain's determination to maintain her naval supremacy and her Ententes with France and Russia stood in her way. Talk of an Anglo-German *rapprochement* was anathema to Crowe, who regarded German promises as entirely untrustworthy, designed to lull the British into a false sense of security while Germany completed her naval and military preparations. Crowe's famous memorandum of 1 January 1907 was the first full-length exposition of his views,[52] and while Salisbury would never have tolerated such an effusion from a relatively minor official, Grey and Hardinge praised it. For the most part however Grey ignored Crowe's advice, while perhaps accepting some of his assumptions. Crowe's outspokenness, his contempt for politicians, and his extremism worked against him. Grey tended to rely on the more flexible Hardinge—the two men became extremely friendly—who, like Grey, tended to concentrate later on Germany's naval rivalry as the chief impediment to better relations between the two countries, a view which Crowe strenuously resisted.

The outgoing Permanent Under-Secretary, Sir Thomas Sanderson, who had served under Salisbury, and who was more tolerant of Germany than his successors, had long been alarmed by the growing anti-Germanism of his colleagues; but his efforts to counteract this tendency earned him only the obloquys of the Bertie-Hardinge group, while accomplishing little. With his departure the anti-Germans were given full rein, although as Grey became more experienced their influence tended to diminish. By

1908 the senior posts at home and abroad were monopolized by this group. In that year Hardinge secured the retirement of Sir Frank Lascelles, who had been ambassador at Berlin since 1895, and was a friend of the German Emperor and much criticized in the Foreign Office minutes after 1906 for being too ready to see the German point of view. After some confusion he was replaced by Sir Edward Goschen, the British Ambassador at Vienna, and a firm believer in the maintenance of the Ententes. His place in Vienna was taken by Sir Fairfax Cartwright, the Minister at Munich, whose despatches from Bavaria had been distinguished by an incredible suspicion of Germany, and, as such, were much praised by Crowe and the others.

The major issue facing the new Foreign Secretary was the prospect that the forthcoming conference at Algeçiras was likely to lead to a recrudescence of Franco-German tension. Grey had already emphasized in opposition that while the Liberals would seek friendship with all countries, including Germany, this must not be at the expense of the Entente with France.[53] He realized that the Germans believed that the Liberals would be less scrupulous than the Unionists had been in upholding England's treaty obligations to France and he was determined to combat this assumption. Thus he went further—but only slightly further—than Lansdowne in gestures of support for France. He informed Metternich on 3 January 1906 that British public opinion would not, in his opinion, 'leave the French Government in the lurch' if war broke out between France and Germany over Morocco. When on 10 and 31 January the anxious Cambon enquired of Grey whether the British Government would back her diplomatic support of France by force if necessary, Grey replied on the second occasion that while the Cabinet was not prepared to give a formal declaration or to agree to an alliance, he personally felt that if Germany forced war on France, British public opinion would not allow Great Britain to remain neutral. Lansdowne, suspicious of France after Delcassé's fall, had never given the French such an assurance; nevertheless Grey's statement was so hedged about with qualifications and reservations as to discourage France from adopting an incautious attitude in her dealings with Germany at the conference. During the conference Grey was under strong pressure from Bertie, Mallet and Cambon and the others to offer France an alliance in order to prevent France, in her weakness, from drifting into Germany's arms. Grey's response was always the same—that the Cabinet and country would not tolerate the sort of alliance with continental Powers that had been contemplated in Joseph Chamberlain's day.

Nevertheless, Grey did agree on 10 January to unofficial conversations between General Grierson of the War Office and Colonel Huguet, the French Military Attaché, to discuss the means by which the French and British armies could co-operate in the event of a war with Germany. These conversations were a logical outcome of the debate about the best methods of assisting France militarily and navally which had been considered by the War Office and Admiralty since the previous year. Early in 1906 senior British army officers had recommended that the despatch of 100,000 British troops to France in the event of war would be of more value to the French than the Admiralty's plans for lightning military-naval raids on the German coast. Naturally the army wanted a more prominent role in any continental warfare than the auxiliary one assigned to them by the Admiralty, but the decision also demonstrated the new concentration on European problems after 1905.[54]

Grey's authorization of these talks led subsequently to a long controversy as to the degree of commitment which they implied. His failure to inform the Cabinet about them when it convened after the election on 31 January was especially criticized. The fact remained that Campbell-Bannerman (who also agreed, reluctantly, to the talks) and Grey both made it absolutely clear to the French that they were not to bind either Government to go to the assistance of the other in the event of war—'the communications must be solely provisional and non-committal', Grey insisted on 13 January 1906.[55] If the French chose to ignore these reservations (and there is little evidence that they did not), that was their own affair. Grey informed the Cabinet about the talks in 1911 and it was agreed then that they should continue, subject to the same qualification that Grey had made in 1906. Grey admitted later that he had made a mistake in not informing the Cabinet about the conversations in 1906; nevertheless it is difficult to understand why his protestations about the difficult circumstances which prevailed in January 1906 cannot be accepted at their face value.

Grey faced not only a serious continental crisis but also a bitter election campaign. Ministers were fighting for their constituencies, and Grey might well have thought that they would hardly welcome telegrams from the Foreign Office asking for their agreement to the holding of military conversations to discuss measures to meet contingencies that might never arise. Grey regarded the conversations as a technical matter in no way binding on the Government, and in these circumstances, may have decided against placing the matter before the new Cabinet on 31 January, faced as it was by the need to discuss the heavy programme of domestic reform which the Liberal electors had been promised. Furthermore, neither Campbell-Bannerman nor Lord Ripon (the Lord Privy Seal, who was also informed about the talks) raised the subject in the Cabinet, and these two men had had previous Cabinet experience, which Grey lacked.[56] As has already been shown, the practice of referring every matter to the Cabinet had been discouraged by Salisbury and Rosebery—the Cabinet was too cumbersome and awkward a body to handle foreign affairs competently.[57]

The Algeciras conference opened on 16 January 1906. Grey insisted that Britain should help France to secure the special position in Morocco which the Anglo-French convention promised her, for, as he wrote to Arthur Nicolson, the British representative at Algeciras, in December, 1905, 'if she fails the prestige of the Entente will suffer and its vitality will be diminished'.[58] The Germans were equally determined that France's special position in Morocco should not be confirmed by the conference. The rivalry between the two countries soon narrowed to two issues—the state bank, and the control of the police at the Moorish ports. Germany demanded that these two organs should be internationalized, while France urged that she should be given a preponderant voice in both. By 3 March the conference was faced with deadlock on the police question. On that day Germany proposed that the police question should be shelved *pro tem.*, but much to her surprise she found herself outvoted by ten votes to three.[59] Germany yielded, and on 6 March inspired an Austrian compromise whereby France and Spain should control the police at all the ports except Casablanca, whose police should be under a neutral inspector-general, who should supervise the police at the other ports. Nicolson was delighted—'The Germans have been wonderfully conciliatory,' he wrote,[60] and he was correspondingly irritated when France rejected it. The French suspected that Germany would eventually try to secure Casablanca for herself, but Hardinge and Nicolson thought that they were being unreasonable. Grey, however, in his anxiety to maintain the Entente, was not prepared to press the French too far to accept the compromise, although at first he too had regarded the German offer as a real concession.

As early as 9 January 1906 the Foreign Secretary had meditated a scheme whereby, in return for German recognition of French predominance in Morocco, France should concede a port on the Moroccan Atlantic coast to Germany; indeed the very plan that Rouvier had drawn up in 1905, and to which Lansdowne had so much objected. However, Grey dropped the idea in February in the face of French objections. He commented in March that 'cordial co-operation with France in all parts of the world remains a cardinal point of British policy and in some respects we have carried it further than the late Government here was required to do'.[61] Thus, for the same reason, Grey decided to support the French objections to the Austrian compromise, especially when he learnt of a German-inspired rumour that Britain was planning to desert France—'it was their game to sow distrust if they could', he wrote later.[62] On 18 March the Germans gave way and accepted a compromise Austro-American solution. The Act of Algeciras was signed on 7 April 1906. The police in the Moorish ports, including Casablanca, were placed under Franco-Spanish officers, and a Swiss inspector-general was to supply reports on the police to the diplomatic body at Tangier. The state bank was to be open to the capital of all nations, with a special concession to the French. Provisions for the open door to trade in Morocco and public tenders for all concessions were also embodied in the Act.[63]

The Entente had won a notable diplomatic victory, while Germany had been isolated, an outcome for which she could blame only her own blundering diplomacy, which had driven France and England closer together. Grey's suspicions about Germany's aims and methods were inevitably sharpened by her attitude before and during the conference. Thereafter, he clung to the Entente as a means of protection against Germany, although at the same time, like Lansdowne, he recognized that France was a somewhat weak reed upon which to lean. This knowledge, however, made Grey even more determined to ensure that France should be given no grounds to suspect that Britain's loyalty to the Entente was in any way weakening, lest this fear should cause France to seek an agreement with Germany. In December 1905 he wrote to Theodore Roosevelt that:

> We wish to keep and strengthen the Entente with France, who is now very peaceful and neither aggressive nor restless . . . The weak point is that she might some day have a scare that we intended to change . . . If . . . by some misfortune or blunder our Entente were to be broken up, France will have to make her own terms with Germany. And Germany will again be in a position to keep us on bad terms with France and Russia, and to make herself predominant upon the Continent. Then, sooner or later, there will be war between us and Germany . . . [64]

Grey rejected arguments that Germany's annexation of Alsace-Lorraine 'has made a combination between France and Germany against us impossible',[65] and that therefore Britain could afford to take a line more independent of France. He believed that French politicians like Rouvier, Caillaux and Étienne were only waiting for an opportunity to take France over to the German camp.

During the next few years Grey strove to convince the French of British loyalty in the face of frequent German newspaper talk of an Anglo-German *rapprochement*, of frequent visits to England by German burgomasters and newspaper editors, and of efforts by the King and Haldane to improve Anglo-German relations. He commented later that 'there was always the risk that these friendly demonstrations . . . might be misrepresented and used at Paris to create distrust.'[66] He deluged the French with assurances when the King visited the German Emperor at Cronberg in August 1906 and again at Wilhelmshöhe in August 1907; and when Haldane visited the German army manoeuvres in September 1906, met the Emperor and nearly became involved in the German celebrations to commemorate Sedan. Grey threatened to resign if these visits led to an Anglo-French estrangement, but although they reconciled the two monarchs, they had little long-term political effect, especially as the naval issue was soon to become a serious question dividing the two countries. Nevertheless, Grey remained alert. In October 1907, after an argument with the King and with Haldane, he secured the abandonment of a proposed visit of the band of the Coldstream Guards to Germany on the grounds that the Army Council had previously turned down a similar invitation for the band to visit France.[67] He also tried to mitigate the possible effects on French opinion of a return visit by William II to Windsor in November 1907 by insisting that Bülow should not accompany the Emperor, and by escaping to Hampshire during the visit, leaving Haldane to act as intermediary between the King and the Emperor.

Nor did he show much concern at the failure of France to honour her side of the convention. Bertie and Crowe were always complaining about persistent French hostility and unhelpfulness towards British interests in Morocco, Newfoundland, Abyssinia, in the Persian Gulf, in Constantinople and in Egypt—indeed in May 1908, Eldon Gorst, Cromer's successor at Cairo, complained that 'the French continue to be very tiresome locally. As is always the case with them the entente as worked in practice is all fair words without performance.'[68] Grey usually took a lenient view of French failings in these matters. He was not greatly interested in imperial problems[69] and was prepared, if necessary, to play them down in the interests of preserving the Entente in Europe. He also felt that France had received a bad bargain over Morocco; at the same time he found commercial questions tedious. British traders and merchants abroad were always complaining that they received little assistance either from the Government at home or from British diplomatic missions.[70] Crowe thought that British capitalists were reluctant to invest in areas of political importance to their country, 'largely because former experiences have left behind an impression that our interests are not pushed with that unscrupulous energy which is characteristic of French and German Government support to concessionaires in foreign countries'.[71]

In the same way Grey was not prepared to resist German efforts to secure coaling stations and ports in various parts of the world, except in the Persian Gulf. In January 1906 he wrote to the Prime Minister that:

> In more than one part of the world I find that Germany is feeling after a coaling station or a port. Everywhere we block this. I am not an expert in naval strategy, but I doubt whether it is important to us to prevent Germany getting ports at a distance from her base; and the moment may come when a timely admission that it is not a

cardinal object of British policy to prevent her having such a port may have a pacific effect.[72]

The example of Morocco has already been mentioned, but he took the same attitude towards German aspirations to a port on the Portuguese African coast. He informed Lord Crewe, the Colonial Secretary, in 1908, that:

> To object to everything unconditionally . . . would be so churlish a policy and would justify them in saying that we were really unfriendly and that their efforts to build a fleet against us must be increased.[73]

Grey's policy was thus not designed to provoke Germany. Hence he always rejected suggestions that he should strive to weaken Germany's position in Europe by attracting one or the other of her allies into the Triple Entente. He believed that this might lead to war; furthermore the Foreign Office wanted the Triple Alliance to continue in its existing weak state, with Italy distrustful of Germany and hostile towards Austria, and, on the other hand, friendly towards France and England. Grey wrote in 1909 that 'the real isolation of Germany would mean war; so would the domination of Germany in Europe. There is a fairly wide course between the two extremes in which European politics should steer.'[74] In the same way he refused to heed advice that he should take active steps to counter German economic and political penetration of the countries on her borders—Sweden, Denmark, Holland, Belgium and Switzerland—which his officials regarded with almost hysterical alarm. He did not view these developments with much concern, believing that they were a natural outcome of Germany's close proximity to those countries. All he asked of them was that they should remain neutral in wartime. Grey restricted British involvement in the affairs of other countries to Portugal, Turkey, Persia and the Gulf. In these areas he was convinced that German preponderance would become a danger to British interests. Otherwise the preservation of the Ententes with France and, later, with Russia, and the maintenance of British naval supremacy would, he believed, be sufficient to deter Germany from adopting aggressive policies.

Between 1906 and 1912 Grey was faced with the same problem in Europe as was Salisbury in the early 1870s, when he had regarded Germany as the only real potential threat to England in view of the comparative weakness of France and Russia.[75] This time Grey sought to align Russia, France and England in a defensive combination which, if necessary, could resist any aspirations by Germany to European hegemony. France and Britain had now settled their differences and, as a result of the Moroccan crisis, had drawn closer together. Now Grey hoped to reach agreement with Russia, and to prevent her, in her weakness, from drifting into Germany's arms. The triangle would then be complete.

Chapter 2

Britain, France and Germany, 1908–12

> The French are not always pleasant bed-fellows but we
> might go further (viz. to Berlin) and fare worse.
>
> *Sir Francis Bertie*, February 1909

Introduction: Anglo-German Naval Rivalry and the Hague Conference

The naval question did not become a really serious issue in the relations between Germany and England until 1908. Grey tended, at first, to ignore the question—he wrote on 1 January 1906 that 'we don't regard their building as a hostile act against ourselves'.[1] By 1908, however, German competition had become so intense that Grey now regarded it as 'the one subject of interest to the exclusion of all other questions' between the two countries.[2] Of course the Admiralty had become concerned much earlier about the implications for future British naval policy of the growth of an efficient German fleet. The Board faced the expensive prospect of coping with the fleets of Germany, France, and Russia, as well as those of the United States and Japan. It also had to consider the purposes behind the German decision to build a fleet. Despite the German claim that her navy was intended for colonial and commerce protection, the Admiralty noted that the German fleet was almost entirely concentrated in home waters and that it was composed mainly of large warships which were unsuitable for the purpose proclaimed by the German Marine Ministry.

The Admiralty was even more alarmed when in 1905 Germany introduced a supplementary law further increasing the size of her fleet. Before he left office the Unionist First Lord, Lord Cawdor, drew up a long-term naval construction programme which provided for the laying down of four large armoured ships a year by England. This was intended to take into account the future pace of technological change in this field, which would render many existing British battleships obsolete, as much as the future progress of German construction. British difficulties were increased when on 10 February 1906 a new battleship—H.M.S. *Dreadnought* —was launched at Portsmouth. The new battleship was faster, better armoured, and larger than any other ship afloat, but at the same time it destroyed England's predominance over Germany by rendering all existing battleships obsolete, since Germany could now compete with England on equal terms. In the short run of course England still possessed overwhelming superiority in pre-Dreadnought battleships, and in any case Admiral Fisher, the first Sea Lord after 1904, argued that, since Germany and other nations were planning battleships, it was an advantage for England to be the first in the field. The net result, however, was to increase the sense of insecurity in England; even Grey thought later that 'we built it and boomed it unnecessarily'.[3]

The Liberals, pledged as they were to reductions in defence expenditure, were unwilling to contemplate the increases in naval expenditure required under the Cawdor programme, and many argued that in any case the disappearance of the Russian fleet rendered such increases unnecessary. Lord Tweedmouth, the First Lord of the Admiralty, therefore announced that only three of the battleships provided for by Cawdor would be required in the 1906–7 estimates, and later the Government decided to postpone a further battleship as a gesture to the second Hague Peace Conference, which was to meet in 1907.[4]

The Prime Minister hoped that the conference would result in a multilateral agreement in the reduction of armaments, but William II and Bülow refused to allow the German delegates to participate in discussions at the Hague on arms limitation. Grey and his officials, never very sanguine about the prospects for the conference, hoped that Germany's attitude would saddle her with the odium for the failure of the conference in the eyes of British and foreign opinion. Grey commented that 'he [the German Emperor] can, if the Reichstag voted the money, oblige us to add another ten or twenty millions to the Navy Estimates in the next few years, but if this is done, I want people here and in Germany who will have to vote the money to realise that it is he who had forced our hand in spite of our wish to limit expenditure.'[5] As a result of Germany's obstructive tactics, the conference (15 June–18 October 1907), achieved only the passage of pious resolutions. The Foreign Office was alarmed that even England's supposed friends, France and Russia, supported Germany at the conference.[6] Eyre Crowe complained to Sir Charles Dilke that 'the most marked feature of the Conference, to my mind, had been the open hegemony exercised by Germany over the States of Europe',[7] while Lord Reay, one of the British delegates, commented gloomily that 'instead of encouraging disarmament the Conference has certainly increased the existing feeling on the Continent of Europe that no power can afford to neglect its means of offence and defence'.[8]

Anglo-German Negotiations, 1908–11

With the failure of the Hague Conference, and the publication by the German Government, towards the end of 1907, of a further supplementary naval law (novelle), both the British Admiralty and public opinion became seriously exercised by the growth and development of the German navy. The British saw it as a direct threat to their security, unnecessary as a form of defence in view of the large and efficient German army. Eyre Crowe and the others were convinced that the German fleet was intended as an instrument of aggression against the United Kingdom; the anti-Germans now had a more tangible example of German hostility on which they could vent their feelings. The Admiralty demanded an increase in the British estimates to compensate for the new German programme, a demand which led to the first of a series of disputes in the Cabinet over naval questions, which at times seriously strained the unity of the Government.

Surprisingly, Grey had faced little Cabinet opposition to his policy before 1908. It might have been expected that the pro-Boers would have taken a keen interest in overseas developments and especially in the growing British alignment with France and her steady drift away from Germany. However, those Liberal Ministers who later expressed concern about the growing rift between England and Germany—James Bryce, Lloyd George, Lord Loreburn (the Lord Chancellor), John Burns, and Lewis Harcourt—took little interest in foreign affairs before 1908 and were in any case preoccupied with the programme of social reforms with which, as Ministers in charge of home affairs, they were chiefly concerned. Furthermore, there were no startling crises in foreign policy after 1906. Grey's policy was pacific, and the reforms of Admiral Fisher in the navy and Haldane in the army had enabled the Government to reduce the service estimates. Grey tended to confide only in a small group of Ministers who were interested in, or concerned with, foreign affairs—Lord Ripon, Haldane and John Morley (Secretary for India) as well as Campbell-Bannerman. Haldane, as has been suggested, made occasional efforts to improve Anglo-German relations, but these were unavailing, and he received little support from Campbell-Bannerman and the other pro-Boers, who disliked him.[9] Asquith, as Chancellor of the Exchequer, was not much concerned with foreign affairs and, like Haldane, was a close friend of Grey. Morley occasionally complained about the anti-Germanism of the foreign office—he wrote in 1908 that 'I don't belong to the Potsdam Party. But then no more do I belong to the Excitables, who . . . are forever smelling out German machinations'[10]—but he was immersed in Indian problems and in any case supported Grey's efforts to reach agreement with Russia.[11]

In 1908, as in future years, a rupture over the estimates was avoided by a compromise, but the Cabinet naval 'economists' quickly perceived that since the Admiralty justified its proposals for naval increases on the grounds of intense German competition, a solution to the problem might be found in the improvement of Anglo-German relations. Grey's difficulties really began in April 1908, when Asquith replaced the ailing Campbell-Bannerman at No. 10 Downing Street, and David Lloyd George and Winston Churchill were promoted to the Exchequer and the Board of Trade respectively. These two soon became staunch allies in a campaign to secure reduced naval estimates, which, they averred, could be achieved by agreement with Germany. They justified their campaign by reference to Liberal election pledges—that Liberal supporters expected that savings in the service estimates would be devoted to the task of social reform. The two men began to exasperate Grey and his officials, not only by delivering speeches up and down the country advocating an Anglo-German naval agreement, but also by making direct approaches to the Germans. Grey and Asquith believed that to reduce the estimates in the face of German competition would be a very dangerous step; in Grey's words, although he advocated retrenchment at the general election, 'I always exempted the Navy from my promises and in any case promises must be subordinated to the national safety.'[12] His officials cordially agreed. They had long regarded

Lloyd George as a Germanophil who would not be sorry to see the Triple Entente disappear in the interest of an agreement with Germany. They did not believe that the Germans would ever agree to genuine reductions—as Crowe put it, 'I believe we must reckon it as a hard fact that whatever the cost, the German Government will build the big and powerful navy . . . which they have so systematically planned.'[13] Hardinge commented that, faced with German competition, Great Britain had no recourse but to construct 'a very large number of battleships'.[14]

Nevertheless, while Grey tended to share these views, he could see the advantages of a naval agreement with Germany, provided it left British naval supremacy intact. A naval agreement would end the annual rumpus over the naval estimates so dangerous to Liberal unity, assuage Liberal opinion in the country, and contribute to the relaxation of international tension. Thus, while dubious about the prospects, he made two approaches to the Germans in 1908, when, accompanied by Lloyd George, he approached Metternich in July to suggest mutual reductions in shipbuilding programmes, and again in August, through the medium of Hardinge, when the latter accompanied the King on a visit to the German Emperor at Cronberg. Neither effort elicited a response. William II refused to discuss a naval agreement, and expressed irritation at being approached. Accordingly Grey decided to desist for the time being from further attempts to secure an understanding, since these appeared to embarrass the German Government, and exacerbate relations between the two countries.

This decision was lost on the ebullient Lloyd George who persisted in his campaign for an agreement.[15] Lloyd George visited Germany in August to study German old age pensions, and he soon began to proclaim publicly his willingness to meet German leaders to discuss the naval question. Grey became agitated that the French might suspect that Britain was meditating some deal with Germany at the expense of French interests, and on 22 August he wrote to Asquith that:

> it is very risky for Cabinet Ministers to go abroad and make utterances about international affairs when they are out of touch with the F[oreign] O[ffice]. I shall make no fuss as long as no harm is done, but if any harm was done I should have to insist on the Minister in question being disavowed which would be humiliating for him, or

33

on my resignation being accepted, which would cause inconvenience.[16]

Accordingly Asquith, equally dismayed, ordered Lloyd George to desist from his efforts; this was in fact unnecessary as the Chancellor of the Exchequer had little success in Berlin.

Thus in 1908 those Ministers 'who only hear or believe in the soft side of German opinion'[17] failed to make any headway in their campaign for an agreement with Germany. Anglo-German relations deteriorated further during the winter of 1908/9 as a result of the German Emperor's extraordinary outburst in the *Daily Telegraph*, a serious dispute between France and Germany over some German deserters from the French Foreign Legion at Casablanca, and finally the long drawn-out Bosnian crisis. These developments naturally increased Grey's suspicions of German diplomacy—'she has reached that dangerous point of strength which makes her itch to dominate',[18] he wrote in November 1908. The atmosphere was further embittered when towards the end of 1908 the Admiralty revealed its suspicions that the Germans were secretly accelerating their naval construction programme. There was another tussle in the Cabinet when the Admiralty demanded the construction of an additional six dreadnoughts as the minimum necessary to combat the German manoeuvre, while the economists contended that only four were required. The alarm soon spread to the country, and the ensuing naval scare, in which exaggerated rumours of Germany's naval capabilities were freely bandied about, led to angry exchanges between Grey and Metternich, to the further detriment of Anglo-German relations. Eventually the First Lord, Reginald McKenna, supported by Grey and Asquith, routed the economists and by the famous compromise, whereby four were to be laid immediately and four later if necessary, eventually secured eight dreadnoughts, two more than he had originally demanded.[19]

Given this inauspicious atmosphere the Foreign Office was considerably surprised, as well as alarmed, when German newspapers and officials began to put forward suggestions during the spring for an Anglo-German naval and political agreement. Such proposals were unwelcome at this time to Grey and his officials, who wanted to concentrate on repairing the Triple Entente after the strains of the Balkan crisis. They suspected that Germany's approaches were designed to undermine further Britain's relations with France and Russia, as well as to encourage the Cabinet economists to demand cuts in the British estimates. 'We need a little breathing time in foreign affairs just now,' Grey told Churchill in April, 'and I think the risk of a new departure is greater than its advantage at the moment.'[20] He thought that an Anglo-German entente would merely 'serve to establish German hegemony in Europe and would not last long after it had served its purpose.'[21]

Nevertheless, as the German campaign showed no sign of diminishing during the summer, Grey, Asquith and Hardinge realized that they could not hope to ignore Germany's approaches indefinitely, especially as the radicals in and out of Parliament were beginning to respond to the clamour in Germany and, since as Hardinge put it, the naval question 'loomed like a heavy cloud over the relations between the two countries'.[22] Thus Grey gave a cautious welcome to a suggestion by the new German chancellor, Theobald von Bethmann Hollweg, on 21 August, that the two countries should open negotiations for a naval and political agreement. There ensued two years of fruitless negotiations. Grey's officials, other than Hardinge, were totally opposed to his more flexible attitude to Germany's approaches, which, they were convinced, were designed to undermine the Ententes. Grey himself lost all confidence in the prospects for the negotiations when the Germans refused to cut their existing naval programme and would offer only a relaxation in the 'tempo', or pace of construction, of their battleships, a proposal which, as Hardinge pointed out, offered no long run savings to the British Exchequer. Coupled with this niggardly gesture was a German demand for a 'political formula', designed to demonstrate to the world that the two countries were now reconciled. Grey's subordinates lost no time in attacking this plan as a clear attempt to separate Britain and France. Although Grey continued to emphasize to the Germans that British public opinion regarded the reduction of naval expenditure 'as *the* test of whether an understanding is worth anything',[23] Bethmann, on 10 April 1910, withdrew even his limited naval offer and proposed instead a neutrality and non-aggression pact which would, he claimed, so improve relations between the two countries as to make a naval agreement unnecessary.

Grey told the Cabinet on 20 July 1910 that England could not enter into such an agreement, which would certainly result in the loss of Franco-Russian friendship. He persuaded the Cabinet to agree to a British counter-memorandum which insisted that a naval agreement was the only means of reducing tension between the two countries. Bethmann however continued to insist on a political agreement. Sir Arthur Nicolson, who replaced Hardinge as Permanent Under-Secretary in the autumn of 1910, summed up Foreign Office opinion in October when he wrote to Goschen that, 'I have little belief that, in the question of naval armaments or political understandings, any results will be obtained,'[24] a view which Grey and Asquith now shared.

The economists, however, were of a different opinion. Lloyd George and Lord Loreburn had already exhibited signs of impatience at the dilatory pace of the negotiations, which was in fact caused by delays on the German side and the two British general elections in 1910, as much as by Grey's lack of confidence in the discussions. Angered by further increases in the 1911–12 naval estimates, which they had been unable to prevent, and assisted by a radical Liberal campaign in press and Parliament against the allegedly anti-German orientation of British foreign policy, the economists persuaded the Cabinet, in January 1911, to set up a committee on foreign affairs, consisting of Asquith, Grey, Lord Crewe, Morley, Lloyd George and Walter Runciman, the President of the Board of Education. The committee was set up in answer to Lloyd George's complaints about lack of information about foreign policy; but while it saw papers on other subjects, there can be little doubt that its main purpose was to hasten progress towards an agreement with Germany.

Certainly this was the view of the Foreign Office, and throughout its brief period of existence, Nicolson and the others were terrified that the committee would force Grey to accept an agreement with Germany which would upset the Ententes. In fact only Lloyd George can be regarded as a staunch critic of Grey's policy on the committee, and while the Chancellor of the Exchequer made many proposals, Grey defeated an effort by the committee to emphasize the importance of a political over a naval agreement. Eventually Grey won a clear victory, for the Cabinet, in accepting, on 8 March, a draft memorandum of new proposals to the Germans from the committee, insisted that a naval agreement must form an essential part of any Anglo-German agreement, and that any political formula must be so worded that it could not possibly be misinterpreted in France or Russia.[25]

On 9 May, however, Bethmann once more emphasized the primacy of a political understanding over a naval agreement. The views of the two Governments were thus as far apart as they had been in 1909, and a genuine reconciliation was, under the circumstances, impossible. The Cabinet thereafter concentrated, down to the early summer, on trying to settle an agreement for an exchange of naval information between the two countries, a scheme which Grey had put forward earlier in the negotiations as another method of reducing mutual suspicions. To the intense relief of Grey's officials, who had continued to fear that the Cabinet might give way to Germany's pressure, the Agadir crisis put an end both to the discussions between the two countries, and to the committee on foreign affairs.

The Agadir Crisis

Between 9 February 1909, when Germany and France signed an agreement providing for mutual economic co-operation in Morocco, and July 1911, there was a relaxation in tension between these two countries. These years were dominated by the naval rivalry between Germany and England and, in view of their suspicions of Germany, the Foreign Office staff regarded France's co-operation with that power in Morocco as less than loyal to her Entente associate. Unfortunately the *raison d'être* of the Entente was political and not economic, and French financiers pursued their interests in Morocco and elsewhere with little regard for British commercial interests.[26] Thus between 1909 and 1911 French and German financiers and concessionaires tried to monopolize Moroccan trade and mineral resources, to the exclusion of their British counterparts. The Foreign Office files of this period were full of complaints about the grasping nature of the French in these matters. Hardinge summed up the general feeling in January 1909, 'how difficult it is to work with the French who never seem to act in a straightforward manner'.[27] Moreover French assertiveness in Morocco threatened to drive Spain into Germany's arms. Grey had secured Spain's adhesion to the Entente camp when, on 16 May 1907, he had negotiated an agreement between Britain, France and Spain to preserve the status quo on the Mediterranean and neighbouring Atlantic coasts (including Gibraltar), and providing for tripartite consultations if the status quo were threatened by a fourth Power.[28] After 1908, however, France seemed bent on destroying this flimsy accord by attempting to minimize Spain's rights in areas of Morocco assigned to her under the Franco-Spanish convention of 1904. Spain naturally resented this, and at the same time, in anticipation of the break-up of the country, attempted to secure, by means of economic penetration and by military advances, as much as possible of the regions pledged to her in 1904. The British attempted to mediate between the two countries: while they were not prepared 'to throw the French overboard to please Spain',[29] they recognized that some of Spain's complaints were justified, especially as they were equally irritated by French policy in Morocco.

Britain's troubles with France were not confined to Morocco. In Newfoundland the French attempted to recede from the agreement about fishing rights which had been concluded in 1904. Eyre Crowe penned scathing minutes about their unfriendly attitude and in 1911, he wrote that if, in 1904, the British had any inkling of the interpretation France would place on the Newfoundland convention, 'the whole negotiation would have been broken off and the Entente never concluded'.[30] The British were also angry with the French for refusing to terminate their right to trade arms in Muscat (which were flowing into Afghanistan and falling into the hands of hostile tribesmen on the Indian frontier), unless the British would cede the Gambia, a suggestion which the Cabinet rejected in 1909.[31] French persecution of Protestant missionaries in Madagascar provoked Grey to exclaim in 1912, that 'this might become the most serious danger to our friendship with France. It may mobilise all the feeling of the United Churches of Great Britain. . . . No policy can stand in this country if it appeared to be on the side of secular intolerance against Christianity.'[32] In 1911 Lord Crewe remarked that, 'it is one of the least satisfactory features of the Entente, which has several not too satisfactory, that we do not seem to get much more help from their Government in matters of this sort than if we were still wrestling at Cairo or if Marchand had just reached Fashoda',[33] and a year earlier Hardinge complained that the French 'like to be paid twice over for any concession that they make by agreement with us'.[34]

As has already been pointed out, Grey was unwilling to make a serious issue of these difficulties since he was convinced that 'unless we had the Entente we should be isolated and might have everybody against us'.[35] The Entente was a rather negative and defensive combination whose purposes were never clearly defined, at least by Grey, who consistently refused to give France any long-term assurances of British support in case of a German attack upon her. Under the circumstances he was unlikely to play into Germany's hands by quarrelling with France over colonial and economic questions, which were in any case peripheral to Europe, the main concern of his policy.

Grey managed to preserve the Entente in the lean years between 1909 and 1911 by playing down the colonial disputes, and by paying careful attention to French susceptibilities.[36] Thus the Entente was still intact when, on 1 July 1911, Germany reopened the Moroccan crisis by sending a gunboat to the south Moroccan port of Agadir. Not that Grey had welcomed the French decision, in the spring, to send a military expedition to Fez to rescue European citizens from the revolting subjects of the Sultan, Mulai Hafid.[37] He suspected then that should the French find themselves unable to withdraw, Germany would claim that Algeciras had been breached and would, in Crowe's words, be able to resume their 'traditional policy of blackmail'.[38] The French reached Fez on 21 May 1911 and Germany seemed, for the moment, prepared to accept a temporary French occupation. Nevertheless, Grey hoped that the French would put down the rebellion and leave quickly. His officials, remembering cavalier French treatment of British interests in the past, feared that France, in her anxiety to secure German recognition of a French protectorate over Morocco, would offer her concessions affecting British strategic interests. Grey's main concern was that Germany would secure a Mediterranean port, although, as in 1906, he was not unwilling that she should secure an unfortified port on the south Moroccan coast. He rejected suggestions by Bertie and the French Foreign Minister that he should strengthen French determination to resist German pressure for concessions by tightening Anglo-French naval and military relations.

With the arrival of the *Panther* at Agadir Europe was faced with a new crisis. The German Foreign Minister, Kiderlen Waechter, believed that this dramatic move would demonstrate to the French that Germany was determined to secure compensation should France remain in Morocco. Unfortunately he failed to make it clear to Grey, who had already recognized that Germany was entitled to compensation, what his intentions were, and Germany's 'abrupt'[39] action led the Foreign Office to conclude that Germany was once more trying to humiliate France and smash the Entente. Nicolson and his colleagues urged Grey to take all necessary military and naval measures, including the despatch of a British gunboat to Agadir, to assert Britain's right to be consulted in any settlement of Morocco and to prevent its being divided between France, Germany and Spain to the detriment of British interests. However the Cabinet, which met on 4 July, decided against over-reacting to the affair. Little sympathy was wasted on France, whose actions were felt to have led to Germany's interference, and none of the Ministers, least of all Grey, wanted a war to put France in possession of Morocco. The Cabinet resolved:

(1) that England must be included in any negotiations to determine the future of Morocco.
(2) that although England would stand by her 1904 obligations, it was up to France to make suggestions for the settlement of the dispute.
(3) that Germany must not secure a port on the Mediterranean coast of Morocco.
(4) that Germany might be allowed an unfortified port on the Atlantic coast of Morocco.
(5) that no British gunboat was to be sent to Agadir.

Grey's officials were united in opposition to the course laid down by the Cabinet, a course which they considered to be weak and vacillating. They did not think that any port obtained by Germany would remain unfortified for long. They welcomed, and indeed encouraged, French determination not to concede territory in Morocco to Germany, and they bombarded Grey with minutes and letters urging him to stand firmly by the side of France in resisting German pretensions. All, except Crowe, now believed that France would not willingly grant concessions to Germany in Morocco, but would only do so if she was bullied by Germany and at the same time unsure of British support. As Eric Drummond put it on 13 July, 'so long as the German methods of treating the French remain as brutal as they are, I think that the French will stick to us'.[40]

Grey rejected their advice. He agreed to the opening of separate Franco-German talks at Berlin on 10 July to settle the compensation France should give Germany in return for a French protectorate over Morocco, although he insisted that France should keep England informed of the progress of negotiations, and he reminded her that British economic interests in Morocco must not be infringed. However the crisis took a more serious turn when, in the middle of July, the French informed London that Germany was demanding the whole of the French Congo as compensation for French control of Morocco. Asquith thought this 'a choice specimen of what the Germans call diplomacy',[41] while Crowe minuted that the loss of the Congo 'will mean definitely the subjugation of France' by Germany.[42] The Prime Minister called a Cabinet for 19 July, at which Grey suggested that he should propose a new international conference on Morocco and that, if Germany refused, 'we should take steps to assert and protect British interests'. This was opposed by Lord Loreburn on the grounds that it might easily lead to war. After a long discussion the Cabinet decided to defer any communication to Germany until its next meeting: however it did agree on what should be asked of France. France should be requested to submit her counter-proposals to Germany on the subject of compensation in the French Congo, and was to be told that if she decided to resist '*à l'outrance*' the admission of Germany into Morocco, Britain would not regard it 'as fatal to British interests and it could not be treated by us as a *casus belli*'.[43]

This was hardly the united front against Germany for which the Foreign Office had been clamouring. Crowe expressed his feelings to Bertie on 20 July—'I am sorry beyond words at the line we are taking . . . It seems to me that our Cabinet are all on the run and the strong hints we are giving France that she must let Germany into Morocco makes me ashamed as well as angry.'[44] Grey too was now becoming concerned about developments. He wrote to Asquith after the Cabinet meeting that England's continued silence, after he had relayed the Cabinet's decision of 4 July to Metternich, might lead Germany to increase her demands on France in the belief that England would not interfere. He thought that the time had now come for England to make it clear to Germany that she must be a party to any discussion should the Franco-German negotiations collapse.[45] He wrote to Bertie that 'if Germany is very unreasonable our own interests may require us to take a foremost front position in the controversy . . . and go to extremes if need be.'[46]

The Cabinet met on the morning of 21 July amid increasing international tension and mounting industrial unrest at home. The atmosphere was not improved by the publication in *The Times* on 20 July of exaggerated details of Germany's demands on France. All the Ministers except Loreburn, and possibly Morley and Harcourt, agreed that the time had now come to make a clear statement to Germany about Morocco. The Cabinet resolved that:

> seventeen days had elapsed without any notice being taken by Germany of the British statement of our position; that while we wished well to the negotiations for any arrangement in the Congo or elsewhere, i.e. West Africa, which would be satisfactory to Germany and France, and put an end for the time being at any rate to any question of compensation for Germany in Morocco, yet if that proved impossible, it must be clearly understood that we recognise no settlement of Morocco in which we had not a voice.[47]

Grey's statement to Metternich after this meeting and Lloyd George's famous Mansion House speech in the evening were both in line with this decision. Lloyd George's speech was an independent initiative of his own, taken after consultation with Grey and Asquith.[48] There is little evidence that Lloyd George intended it as a warning to France not to settle Morocco independently of Britain.[49] The Germans were in no doubt that the speech was directed at them, as Metternich's angry protests on 24 July about its tone of provocation demonstrated. This interview led Grey to conclude that Germany had intended to humiliate France and to ignore England, and he caused the fleet to be alerted, for, 'we are dealing with a people who recognise no law except force between nations'.[50]

From Grey's point of view the defection of the supposedly pro-German Lloyd George from the anti-Entente camp had a number of beneficial effects. The speech had more influence on Germany than any comparable effort by Grey would have done; it had convinced France that England would support her; and it had demonstrated to British public opinion that the Cabinet was united, while leaving the other pro-Germans there rather helpless.

Morley and Loreburn repeatedly protested both to Grey and Asquith that the speech was needlessly provocative (Loreburn indeed threatened to resign if Grey did not change the pro-French orientation of his policy) but their complaints produced little beyond a soothing statement to the Commons by Asquith on 27 July 1911. During the summer Asquith, Grey, Haldane, Lloyd George, and Churchill, in a sense usurped the functions of the Cabinet by holding a number of private meetings in Haldane's London house to discuss British policy. Haldane, Churchill, and, later, Lloyd George, were active in ensuring that the country's defences were placed on a war footing. Indeed there is some evidence that the two latter wanted to go further in the matter of preparedness than Grey deemed prudent, suggesting, for instance, alliances between Britain, France and Russia to defend the Low Countries; measures that would be bound to come to the knowledge of Germany and thereby increase the chances of war. Churchill wanted the fleet to move to Scottish waters as a demonstration to Germany that Britain meant business, and:

> where it w[oul]d at once be the most effective and least provocative support to France and a real security to this country. It is not indeed for Belgium, that I w[oul]d take part in this terrible business. One cause alone c[oul]d justify our participation—to prevent France from being trampled down and looted by the Prussian junkers—a disaster ruinous to the world, and swiftly fatal to our country.[51]

It was the enthusiasm of Churchill, and of the energetic Director of Military Operations at the War Office, Sir Henry Wilson, that led Asquith to call a special meeting of the Committee of Imperial Defence on 23 August to discuss possible British strategy in the event of war. The Cabinet dissenters were not invited, and the Government was represented by Asquith, Grey, Lloyd George, Churchill, Haldane and McKenna. While Asquith re-emphasized that it was for the Cabinet to decide whether or not England should come to the aid of France if Germany attacked her, the General Staff recommended that, in this event, a British expeditionary force should be despatched to France and that the task of the navy should be to protect and transport the army. Naturally the Admiralty resented this subordinate role, and McKenna put forward a counter-plan for combined military-naval raids on German ports and off-shore islands. The First Lord, however, was in the minority and despite his warnings that a pledge of British assistance might make France less inclined to accept Germany's terms for a Moroccan settlement, the meeting decided in favour of the War Office's plan to send 166,000 men to the western front in the event of war.[52]

The War Office, unlike the Admiralty, impressed the meeting with its carefully worked-out plans, and McKenna's unhelpful attitude caused Asquith to replace him as First Lord by Churchill in October.[53] The military conversations with France, which had languished since 1906, had already been revived, and plans for joint co-operation worked out by Sir Henry Wilson.[54] In fact a C.I.D. sub-committee had already recommended the despatch of the expeditionary force to France in July 1909.[55] Both the War Office and the Foreign Office believed that, supported only by Russia, who had still not fully recovered from her defeat at the hands of Japan, France was too weak to withstand a German attack without British military, naval, and financial support.[56] Of course, all recognized that British public opinion was more likely to support British intervention if Germany violated Belgian neutrality—although in this event little British assistance could be spared for Belgium.

In the event the military plans and preparations were un-necessary in 1911. The Franco-German negotiations continued during the autumn, punctuated by occasional French cries of alarm about the fluctuating and sometimes excessive nature of Germany's demands. The Franco-German convention of 4 November settled the Moroccan question once and for all. France secured the coveted protectorate over Morocco, while Germany received some compensation in the French Congo, although not as much as Kiderlen would have liked. Germany did not get a foothold in Morocco. That the talks ended successfully was partly a result of Grey's efforts. After Lloyd George's speech he had pressed the French to persist with the conversations at Berlin, and, often against the advice of his officials, he had intervened occasionally to persuade them to make more generous colonial offers to Germany, to prevent them from being the first to break off the negotiations, and from sending a gunboat to Agadir. He was determined that, if Germany deliberately attacked France, or inveigled her into war, England should support France. But he insisted that all peaceful means must be exhausted before Europe was plunged into war. He refused all French requests for a British pledge of assistance, reminded them that British public opinion would require that Germany should be seen as the violator of the peace, secured Cabinet sanction on 31 July to call a conference if the Berlin talks broke down, and even toyed with the idea of invoking the arbitration of President Taft. He thus steered a narrow course between the faint-hearted in the Cabinet, like Loreburn, who wanted absolutely no British involvement in the dispute, and the bellicosity of the Foreign Office, and later of Churchill and Lloyd George, whose ardour he tried to restrain.

By the autumn the Foreign Office was of course delighted with the course of events. Nicolson wrote that 'the French would not flinch from accepting war with Germany' and he was convinced that England would go to her aid. Those former pro-Germans, Haldane, Lloyd George, and Churchill were, he was glad to find, 'perfectly ready—I might almost say eager—to face all possible contingencies'.[57] But Germany's clumsy diplomacy during the crisis failed to have the effect on British public opinion which the Foreign Office anticipated, i.e. to convince all those in favour of closer relations with Germany of the futility and danger of such a course. Towards the end of 1911 radical Liberal newspapers and Parliamentarians mounted a full-scale attack on Grey's foreign policy, claiming that its pro-French orientation had nearly led to an Anglo-German war for the sake of French interests, and calling for a new effort to reach agreement with Germany. The campaign in the country strengthened the hands of the pro-German Cabinet Ministers, Harcourt, Morley and Loreburn, who began to press Grey to reopen the negotiations with Germany which had been suspended since June. McKenna, angered by his transfer from the Admiralty to the Home Office, joined their ranks, and he took up the theme, which he had initiated at the C.I.D. meeting, that the military conversations with France should be examined by the Cabinet. Grey had already become embarrassed early in 1911 by rumours circulating in the foreign and domestic press about the talks. The French had also referred to them during the spring, when they were trying to strengthen the Entente *vis à vis* Germany. One such allusion which appeared in a despatch caused Grey, on 16 April, to inform Asquith about them—for some reason the Prime Minister had never been let in on the secret. Although Asquith was irritated that he had been kept in the dark, he did not stop the talks, although he became concerned in the autumn that they might be encouraging French army chauvinism.

This was the burden of McKenna's complaints to Asquith during the course of a long conversation about his transfer to the Home Office at the Prime Minister's home at Archerfield on 20 October. He feared that Britain might, as a result of the talks, be dragged into war with Germany for the sake of French interests.[58] Morley, piqued by his exclusion from the C.I.D. meeting of 24 August, raised the question of the expediency of such talks taking place without Cabinet sanction at a Cabinet meeting on 1 November 1911. Although Haldane, Asquith and Grey insisted that the conversations in no way prejudiced the right of the Cabinet to decide on questions of war or peace, the majority of the Ministers were plainly alarmed by these clandestine activities. Even the usually moderate Lord Crewe sided with the fifteen Ministers who 'took a strong and decided line about Cabinet supremacy over all other bodies on the matter of land and sea defence'.[59] Only Lloyd George and Churchill supported the other three.

Nevertheless, the dissenters could not carry their opposition too far. As the War Office pointed out, Crewe and McKenna had attended the C.I.D. meeting in 1909 at which future strategy had been worked out. Morley knew something of the conversations as a result of deputizing for Grey at the Foreign Office early in 1911 —and he had not made a fuss then. The non-binding nature of the talks had been repeatedly made clear to the French. Haldane threatened to resign if the talks were stopped, and no doubt Churchill, who urged Grey on the 4th, to take up 'a very strong position about military conversations with the French',[60] would have gone with him. The issue was not in any case worth a breach and, after a prolonged and animated discussion at a second Cabinet meeting on 15 November, the Cabinet adopted a skilful formula drawn up by Asquith which managed to satisfy both sides. The conversations were formally declared to be non-binding on both Governments and required prior Cabinet sanction. Grey was not very happy about the resolution, but Asquith prevailed on him to accept it. Little harm was done by the resolutions. Wilson had already settled with the French plans for British intervention down to the last detail. Informal contracts continued and Churchill was able to secure Cabinet approval in 1912 to the opening of naval conversations with France.

Nevertheless, the Cabinet deliberations on the military conversations must have been a severe shock to Grey suggesting, as they did, the meagre support he could muster in any conflict over foreign policy. Ministers were influenced by the pressure of Liberal opinion, which in turn tended to accept German press and official complaints that Britain's intervention in the Moroccan dispute had been needlessly provoking. Anglo-German relations in the autumn and winter of 1911 were more strained than they had ever been and the Foreign Office was, as a result, filled with the premonition that war between the two countries was inevitable. Lloyd George and Grey met at Aberdeen on 13 September and the two men concluded gloomily that the future portended 'a patched-up peace between France and Germany, violent animosity worked up against us in Germany for the sake of the January elections there, and a large increase in naval expenditure'.[61]

Grey's long speech to the Commons on 27 November was intended to answer the attacks of his critics both at home and in Germany. He denied that Lloyd George's speech had been intended as a threat to Germany, or that there were secret Anglo-French engagements to assist each other in a war. He attacked talk of a return to splendid isolation, and suggested that, with the settlement of the Moroccan dispute, the way was now open for a relaxation of Anglo-German tension. His speech however failed to appease his critics and Grey saw that the only way to pacify them was by an improvement in Anglo-German relations. Perhaps he had also become disenchanted with Britain's Entente friends. For instance, during the autumn France attempted to recoup her losses in the Congo by reducing Spain's sphere of influence in Morocco to its narrowest limits. Grey, while recognizing that Spain ought to give France reasonable compensation for the latter's sacrifices to Germany, refused to be a party to what he regarded as French greed. 'We can have nothing to do with a line that is mean and dishonourable,' he wrote on 8 November, 'we have got to keep France straight in this matter or to part company with her.'[62] Eventually after angry scenes during November between Bertie and Caillaux, the French Prime Minister, the French gave way and moderated their demands on Spain. Spain thus remained in the Entente camp. Evidence of secret intrigues between Caillaux and the Germans during 1911 for a settlement of the Moroccan dispute also came to light at this time, and created a bad impression. Russia's behaviour in Persia was providing Grey's critics with more ammunition. An improvement of relations with Germany would certainly do no harm.

Anglo-German Relations, 1912

An opportunity was presented to Grey by the German invitation, early in January 1912, to Churchill to visit Berlin to discuss Anglo-German problems.[63] Although sceptical of the prospects, Grey and Churchill decided that Haldane, who had been educated at Göttingen University, and who was keenly interested in German philosophy, should go instead.[64] The agenda for the visit was fully discussed by the post Agadir quartet—Grey, Haldane, Churchill and Lloyd George—towards the end of January. Grey insisted that a genuine reconciliation between the two countries required that Germany should recognize England's naval supremacy, and that she should undertake to reduce, or at least not to increase, her existing naval programme. In return, Grey would agree to receive German proposals for 'reciprocal assurances debarring either from joining in aggressive designs or combinations', and would be prepared to discuss ways of satisfying Germany's colonial aspirations.[65]

The prospects for Haldane's mission were not improved when Asquith received information about a proposed new German supplementary naval law. However the Cabinet, on 2 February, decided that Haldane should go to Berlin to 'feel the way' towards an understanding with Germany about naval and other matters.[66] In Berlin, Haldane failed to persuade Bethmann to agree to naval reductions, and all he secured was a vague promise that the Germans would consider a slight relaxation in the tempo of construction of the new German programme. The Chancellor preferred to concentrate on a neutrality agreement. Haldane rejected a German draft formula which enjoined neutrality on either party if the other was involved in a war with a third power, and settled, instead, for one which prohibited new agreements with third powers which conflicted with the obligations imposed on both parties to remain neutral if either became involved in a war in which it was not the aggressor. The Baghdad railway, Persia and colonial concessions to Germany were also discussed.[67]

While Haldane was pleased with the results of his mission, Grey's officials regarded the proceedings at Berlin as a disaster of the first magnitude. The inexperienced Haldane was accused of bungling the negotiations and giving away a lot to Germany without getting much in exchange. Nicolson, Bertie, Goschen and the others were convinced that a political agreement such as Haldane had outlined would spell the end of the Ententes, and that Germany would never agree to genuine naval reductions. They were terrified that the Cabinet would accept Haldane's programme. Crowe summed up the Foreign Office attitude in February:

> It would be a political mistake of the first magnitude to allow the German Government to squeeze concessions out of us and leave them quite free to pursue the policy of carefully preparing their inevitable war against us. If they are really anxious for friendly relations, they must give some tangible proof in the shape of reduced naval provocation.[68]

Grey, however, insisted that the talks should continue, and Bertie was so alarmed that he hurried to London in February in a desperate bid to stave off disaster. He warned Grey of all the dire consequences that would follow the signature of Haldane's political agreement with Germany. To his horror he discovered that even Grey was prepared to consider something of the sort, for the Foreign Secretary asked the Ambassador whether it was likely that Germany would ever attack France. Bertie concluded gloomily: 'The Government are in a hesitating state. The Lord Chancellor, Harcourt and some others are for coming to arrangements with Germany. Grey is wavering.'[69] Bertie also discovered that Lloyd George had now reverted to his former enthusiasm for a naval and colonial settlement with Germany as a means of limiting naval expenditure. The King too was in favour of an agreement.

Churchill on the other hand was the most opposed, while Asquith exhibited some scepticism about the prospects. Churchill had worked out the consequences for the British naval estimates of the German *novelle*, a copy of which Haldane had brought back with him from Berlin. The First Lord commented that 'I cannot feel that any increase, either in ships or men, on the already great scale of the German navy affords a good basis for agreement.'[70] The Germans proposed to create a third naval squadron and build three additional dreadnoughts, which, Churchill calculated, would necessitate Great Britain increasing her naval expenditure by £12–14 millions over the next five years. Although the Cabinet, on 20 February, felt that

> to follow an exchange of pacific and friendly 'formulae' by the introduction in both countries of Estimates showing the large and progressive increase in Naval Expenditure would be justly regarded as an absurdity if not a mockery,

few Ministers wished to saddle England with the odium of breaking off the negotiations, while others were prepared to accept any agreement that would lead to improved relations between the two countries. After much discussion, it was decided that Grey and Haldane should see Metternich to find out whether the *novelle* could not be altered so as to avoid the necessity for heavy increases in the British estimates.[71] On 22 February Metternich promised the two British Ministers that he would try to find out whether the *novelle* could be reduced.

Lewis Harcourt, the Colonial Secretary, and a leading enthusiast for an agreement with Germany, followed up the Haldane-Grey approach to the Ambassador by urging the Counsellor at the German Embassy, Von Kühlmann, to try to persuade Berlin to be more reasonable about the navy law. Failing this, 'I began to despair of the "accord" which I know that he and I so much desired.'[72] On 12 March Metternich informed Haldane that if the British Government offered Germany a non-aggression pact the new fleet law would be withdrawn. The pro-Germans were delighted by this news, and the Cabinet, on 14 March, drew up a draft non-aggression pact. Metternich, however, demanded that it should include a neutrality clause to bind both powers in case of war—a pledge that Grey adamantly refused to contemplate. In the evening of 14 March, Kühlmann warned Harcourt that if Bethmann failed to secure a satisfactory neutrality formula he would be replaced as Chancellor by the Anglophobe Minister of Marine, Tirpitz, who would insist on the full *novelle*. Harcourt was so impressed with the dangers of the situation that he hurried off to see Haldane, and both men then sent for Grey. They tried to persuade Grey to accept such a clause, but Grey again refused. In Harcourt's words:

Grey very stiff: evidently afraid of losing French Entente. I tried to prove to him that neutrality 'declaration' was no more than we had put in our formula. C[oul]d not move Grey . . .[73]

Thus Harcourt's effort failed. Grey refused to go beyond the British formula of 14 March that England would not pursue an aggressive policy towards Germany. A neutrality clause would suggest to France that England would not go to her assistance if Germany tried to crush her—the basic tenet of Grey's foreign policy. At a further Cabinet meeting on 16 March, the pro-Germans secured a slight amendment to the British formula, but nothing of substance.[74] On 19 March the Germans rejected the British formula as inadequate to justify cuts in the new German navy law. On 29 March the Cabinet condemned the German attitude as 'full of equivocation and pitfalls'.[75] The negotiations languished and by the autumn dropped out of sight for ever. In the end, Bethmann remained Chancellor, desiring an Anglo-German agreement yet unable to persuade either William II or Tirpitz to make naval sacrifices—the only means by which the pro-Germans in the Cabinet could secure sufficient support to force Grey to accept a neutrality clause.

Inevitably the virtual collapse of the negotiations was a great relief to Grey's officials, convinced as they were that Germany was once more scheming to wreck the Ententes. Of course, they remained anxious for the future, since even Grey accepted that the 16 March formula remained on offer.[76] Nicolson sighed in April 'there are many elements in the Cabinet who would do anything to obtain the so-called goodwill of Germany'.[77] On 16 April he re-emphasized his view of Britain's position in Europe:

> In fact England is really a factor of great weight either for or against peace, and I think that one of the best guarantees of peace is that we should retain complete liberty of action and not tie our hands in any way or with anybody but always maintain our present close relations with France and Russia.[78]

That Anglo-German relations, despite this setback, continued to improve during 1912, can partly be ascribed to Harcourt's efforts to effect an agreement with Germany to revise the 1898 agreement between the two countries on the Portuguese colonies,[79] which might soon slip from the feeble grasp of Portugal, shaken as she had been by the Revolution of 1910.[80] Harcourt had broached the possibility of such an agreement to Kühlmann in the autumn of 1911, and discussions between them began in earnest in the spring of 1912. Despite the protests of his officials that Harcourt was trespassing on the field of foreign affairs, Grey seemed quite willing to allow the discussions to continue: he was probably only too glad that Harcourt's energies should be distracted from political formulae. Nicolson complained that

> it is rather absurd our dealing with the property of other people, especially of people whose integrity we have more or less undertaken to defend. The '98 Treaty was not a happy transaction but apparently Harcourt is willing to confirm and extend it. He is . . . a most ardent Germanophile.[81]

By 26 May 1912, Harcourt and Kühlmann had hammered out a draft agreement and Grey ignored Foreign Office strictures that it was too favourable to Germany. Although the Cabinet actually approved the draft treaty on 4 June, certain modifications subsequently requested by Grey in order not to offend the French led to further negotiations, which were not terminated until 1913.

Nevertheless, Grey was prepared to hurry the talks along, despite further protests from his officials that the whole transaction was discreditable in view of Britain's alliance obligations to Portugal. When Germany began to press that the Anglo-Portuguese alliance stood in the way of the application of the revised treaty, Grey and Harcourt proposed that the alliance be made terminable, on the lines of that with Japan. When Crowe and the others warned Grey that to offend Portugal might deprive the British navy of her valuable ports and island anchorages in wartime, Grey in turn pointed to the derelict state of Portugal's colonies—'sinks of iniquity'—the continued existence of slavery in Mozambique, which was beginning to attract the attention of British humanitarian and religious bodies, and to Portugal's ill-treatment of her political prisoners. Plainly, if Portugal were not careful, her shortcomings would be used as an excuse to deprive her of her colonies—even Germanophobes like J. St Loe Strachey thought that Germany would be a better colonizer than Portugal.

Britain, France and the Mediterranean

Once again Grey had demonstrated that he was uninterested in imperial questions and that he was quite prepared to reach an agreement with Germany on overseas colonies provided that the Ententes were preserved in Europe. The latter he had secured by the autumn of 1912. Nevertheless, the French had had anxious moments as the Haldane mission was followed by the Anglo-German negotiations in the winter and spring. Primed by Bertie they were vociferous in their objections even to the limited British formula of 16 March. The nationalist, Raymond Poincaré, who became French Prime Minister in January 1912, was determined to counter any Anglo-German declaration, and to strengthen French security, by persuading Grey to extend the Entente. But his efforts, like those of his predecessors, were completely unsuccessful. While France was kept informed about the progress of the Anglo-German negotiations, Grey would not agree to terminate them at France's behest, and he reminded the French of their willingness to negotiate independently with Germany in the past.

That Poincaré was able to secure some form of declaration from the British—albeit a useless one as far as the French were concerned—resulted from Germany's new naval law. Churchill, now becoming one of the most anti-German members of the Cabinet, soon bombarded the Cabinet with alarming memoranda dwelling on the consequences for the British naval estimates of the German programme. He irritated the pro-Germans and pleased the Foreign Office by trumpeting both at Glasgow, on 9 February 1912, when Haldane was in Berlin, and in the Commons in April, his determination to maintain British naval superiority at all costs.

The prospect of further increases in the estimates was hardly likely to appeal to the economists in the Cabinet or to the mass of Liberal opinion in the country. Churchill believed that he could avoid further heavy increases by reviving a scheme he had propounded in March 1911 for the withdrawal of the British battle fleet from the Mediterranean, leaving a small cruiser force as a British presence in that theatre. In future, Churchill suggested, the British dreadnought fleet should be concentrated against Germany in the North Sea, where he believed the decisive naval battle in an Anglo-German war would be fought.[82] The plan found few supporters, even among the Cabinet economists, to whom it was designed to appeal. The Foreign Office protested that a British naval withdrawal would deprive Britain of all her influence in the Mediterranean, with the consequence that Italy, with her ambitious programme of dreadnought construction already under way, might drift further into the arms of Austria and Germany, followed by Turkey and Greece, who were also embarking on naval expansion. The War Office dwelt on the heavy troop reinforcements that would be needed to guard British possessions in the Mediterranean, and the dislocation that the closure of the Suez Canal in war-time would have on the movement of colonial and dominion troops to Europe. The Board of Trade and the Colonial Office concentrated on the increased vulnerability of British merchant shipping to Austrian naval attack.

The Cabinet dissenters found other arguments to disrupt the fulfilment of Churchill's plan. McKenna, equipped with the technical knowledge to dispute Churchill's arguments, and who also remembered Churchill's opposition to his proposals when he (McKenna) was First Lord, took the lead. The gist of McKenna's case was that contained in his memorandum to the Cabinet of 24 June 1912:

> I do not think that I am misinterpreting Mr. Churchill's strategy when I say that an alliance with France is its essential feature. Without such an alliance I cannot think that his naval advisers would recommend the distribution of the fleet which he now proposes.[83]

McKenna claimed that the existing size of the British navy was quite sufficient to deal both with the German fleet *and* defend the Mediterranean: that heavy naval increases and a Mediterranean withdrawal were alike unnecessary. There ensued a long battle of memoranda and Cabinet duels between the two men during the early summer, with Churchill dwelling on the need to withdraw from the Mediterranean and pressing for a 'definite naval arrangement with France without delay', and with McKenna, supported by Morley and Harcourt, stating that an alliance would compel Britain to intervene in a war provoked by France.[84]

McKenna's assumption was a correct one. While reluctant to agree to a British withdrawal from the Mediterranean, the Foreign Office was looking to the possibility of French naval support as a means of assisting England to counter the growth of the Austrian dreadnought fleet, whose construction was adding to Britain's naval difficulties. France had recently started to improve the efficiency of her fleet. Moreover, Nicolson feared that Italy, whose friendship for the Entente he had previously taken for granted, had been so weakened by her Tripoli venture, and so irritated by French hostility during her (Italy's) war with Turkey,[85] that she might decide to strengthen her ties with Germany and Austria, and to extend the provisions of the Triple Alliance to include the Mediterranean. As a result he believed that France would be too weak to face the Triple Alliance navies alone in the Mediterranean—especially with Italy now in occupation of the Aegean islands and Tripoli. Thus the Foreign Office wanted *both* a naval agreement with France and the maintenance of a strong fleet of dreadnoughts in the Mediterranean, while Churchill believed that the first could be a substitute for the second.

There had been informal Anglo-French naval conversations during the autumn of 1911 to discuss co-operation between the two fleets in case of war with Germany, and Churchill had followed these up in the winter by asking the French to discuss detailed arrangements for French naval support in the Mediterranean. In view of the Cabinet resolution of 15 November 1911, he asked the Cabinet, on 16 May 1912, to agree to the continuation of these talks on a more regular basis. No agreement could be reached and the Cabinet adjourned for the Whitsun recess, while Churchill persuaded Asquith to join him on a visit to Malta where he hoped to convert the Prime Minister, 'free from distractions', to his scheme.[86] There the two men were joined by Kitchener, now Consul-General in Egypt, who was opposed on military grounds to the withdrawal of the fleet. Eventually, after much argument, Churchill agreed to leave two, possibly three, battle cruisers in the Mediterranean, plus four cruisers, as well as eight battleships at Gibraltar, to which he was already committed. Kitchener was unable to persuade the First Lord to leave any dreadnoughts in the Mediterranean, and eventually the three men agreed that some arrangement with France was, under these circumstances, essential.[87]

This compromise satisfied neither Churchill's Foreign Office critics, nor the Cabinet dissenters. There were stormy meetings of the Cabinet during June on the Mediterranean question, and eventually on the 27th, it was decided to refer the strategic aspects of the question to the Committee of Imperial Defence. This meeting took place on 4 July, and was attended by Asquith, Haldane, Morley, Lloyd George, Churchill, Sydney Buxton (President of the Board of Trade), McKenna, Crowe, Grey, Seely,[88] Lord Esher, Nicolson, Admiral Fisher and the naval and military chiefs. After a meeting lasting all day, and which consisted of a recapitulation of the views already rehearsed by the various parties in their memoranda, the Committee resolved that:

> there must always be provided a reasonable margin of superior strength ready and available in Home Waters . . . Subject to this we ought to maintain available for Mediterranean purposes and based on a Mediterranean port, a battle fleet equal to a one-Power Mediterranean standard, excluding France.[89]

This decision appeared to be a defeat for Churchill's scheme to withdraw the battle fleet entirely from the Mediterranean and to leave the French to protect British interests there. In fact, this proved to be far from the case. Churchill pointed out that the navy could not hope to provide the eight dreadnoughts which would be required to maintain a one-power standard against Austria until 1915; until then the Admiralty could only station four battle cruisers there. In any case, the Cabinet economists baulked at the addition of four dreadnoughts which Churchill claimed would have to be added immediately to the estimates if the C.I.D. decision was to be carried out.[90] A decision on this question was postponed. Furthermore, some provision had to be made against any possible combination of Italy, Austria, and Turkey. Once again France was the logical partner, and the dissenters were disappointed in their hope that Anglo-French co-operation might be avoided. The whole question was exhaustively discussed by the Cabinet during July, and after much argument, Churchill's holding plans for the Mediterranean were accepted, and further Anglo-French naval conversations approved, subject to the reservations that they were in no way to bind either Government as to their action should war break out.[91]

However, Poincaré was not prepared to accept the prefacing of an Anglo-French naval convention altering the dispositions of both fleets, and drawn up by the Admiralty on 23 July, by such a clause. He, Bertie and Cambon spent the whole summer trying to persuade Grey, Asquith, and Churchill, not only to exclude the clause from the convention, but to make some more positive statement of British intentions should a war break out between France and Germany. Otherwise, Poincaré threatened not to concentrate the French fleet in the Mediterranean. Grey resolutely refused to consider either suggestion. He thought that the Cabinet would reject such a formula as 'something like an alliance' and hinted that Harcourt and the other pro-Germans were in the ascendancy there. All he would do was to give Poincaré a private assurance that he [Grey] would resign if there was any question of abandoning the Ententes, and to suggest that the next war 'would be a general scrimmage in which France would necessarily be with us'.[92] Poincaré rejected these offers as inadequate and Grey departed for his holidays leaving Asquith to cope with the French. Eventually, Asquith agreed to exclude the non-binding clause from the convention, and, on 11 October 1912, to accept, as 'almost a platitude', a suggestion by Cambon for an exchange of notes whereby if either apprehended a threat to the peace they would consult together as to the best means of dealing with the situation.[93] This was rejected by the Cabinet on 30 October as 'vague and open to a variety of construction'.[94] Grey then drew up a draft formula which, while re-emphasizing the non-binding nature of the naval and military conversations and of the disposition of the Anglo-French fleets, pledged that both powers should consult together, if either feared unprovoked attack or a breach of the peace, as to whether the two Governments would act together to preserve peace, and, if so, what measures they would take in common. After further Cabinet discussion the substance of this draft was approved on 21 November and embodied in the Grey-Cambon exchange of notes on 22 and 23 November.[95]

Although the French had finally secured some sort of declaration from the Cabinet, it was not the binding commitment for which they had been pressing. Both Poincaré and Cambon subsequently admitted that they were disappointed by the British formula. It hardly went beyond what Grey had told them so often before. If there was danger to the peace both powers would presumably have discussed likely contingencies in any case: this clause merely stated the obvious. If Harcourt and the other pro-Germans were prepared to accept this formula there can be little doubt that it was harmless from the British point of view. The naval agreement was signed in February 1913 although, as Churchill had prophesied in the previous autumn, the French had already moved their fleet to the Mediterranean. While Grey believed that British security demanded that she should come to the assistance of France if Germany attacked her, the British Government was, after 1912, in no way committed to such a course.

Nevertheless, German naval competition was driving France and England together in a way that could not have been pleasing to the directors of German foreign policy. Nicolson commented in May 1912 that 'it is certainly a triumph for the German navy that she has succeeded in locking up the whole of the British navy in the North Sea'.[96] Since 1900 England had been forced to withdraw her battleships from the Far East, from North America, and from the Mediterranean, and to adopt a one-power standard there, and then not until 1915. Even minor powers like Greece were buying large battleships and Britain could no longer stand the strain. Balfour realized the logic of his country's situation in June 1912 when he advocated a defensive alliance with France. The Liberal Ministers shrank from such a step and thus England oscillated uneasily in Europe—slowly improving her relations with Germany, yet unwilling to draw too closely to her, remaining on close terms with France, and yet not willing to commit herself to co-operation with her in the event of war.

Chapter 3

Anglo-Russian Relations and the Middle East

An Entente with Russia is now possible and it is the thing most to be desired in our foreign policy. It will complete and strengthen the Entente with France and add very much to the comfort and strength of our position.

Grey, 1906

The Anglo-Russian Convention

Grey was able to bring to a successful conclusion the long drawn-out and frequently interrupted negotiations for a settlement with Russia with which Salisbury had toyed[1] and which Lansdowne had pursued so tenaciously. Lansdowne's interest had languished somewhat in the autumn of 1905, largely because of the strength of Britain's position in the Far East, but also because of the increasing distraction of domestic difficulties. Grey brought with him a fresh enthusiasm to the problem—not only would an agreement with Russia round off the Entente with France, it would also help to discourage Russia from drifting into the arms of Germany. There were more practical reasons for an agreement. The problem of dealing with Russia in Central Asia was as vexatious in 1907 as it had been during the 1880s.[2]

India was surrounded by potential enemies—France in Indo-China; Russia in the North. Indeed the agreements with these two countries were justifiable purely on the grounds of the security of India, without any reference to developments in Europe. Of the two Russia was, of course, the greater danger. By 1900 it appeared to London and Calcutta that Russia, taking advantage of England's South African preoccupations, had embarked on a major effort to bring the buffer states of Tibet, Afghanistan and Persia into her sphere of influence. Persia seemed the most likely candidate for a

Russian take-over. During the 1890s Russia had made considerable progress in furthering her interests in the country, whereas
England, distracted by problems elsewhere, and as hamstrung as
ever by shortages of money and men, seemed weak and vacillating by comparison. Russian influence reached its zenith on 30
January 1900, when the energetic Russian Minister of Finance,
Count Witte, agreed to lend Persia £2½ million based on the
security of all the Persian Customs, except those of the Persian
Gulf. No new foreign loan was to be contracted with third powers
without Russian permission, and until the Russian loan was extinguished. It was evident that the loan would give Russia a large
measure of political and economic control over Persia.[3] By this
time England was even less capable than hitherto of embarking
on a determined policy to counter Russian advances in Persia.
Witte proposed to profit from England's South African difficulties
by making further gains in Persia and Central Asia. He intended
to extract economic concessions from Persia in the form of high-
ways, an oil pipe line, and a more favourable commercial treaty
(which she secured in 1901). England's strategic and political
monopoly in the Persian Gulf was to be challenged by subsidized
Russian steamer services, Russian consulates at major centres
along the Gulf, and perhaps even a Russian naval base.[4]

Equally alarming to the British was the Russian decision in
1900 to try to enter into direct relations with the Amir of Afghanistan, whose foreign relations were, under a treaty of 1880, the
exclusive concern of England. The British were also anxious
about Tibet which, before 1900, they had largely ignored. They regarded the country as part of China, and referred any problems
concerning it to Peking. However by the end of the nineteenth
century, the ruler, the Dalai Lama, sought to throw off the remaining vestiges of Chinese authority, and to make himself fully independent. Reports of various contacts between the Dalai and
Russia in 1900 and 1901 led the Indian Government to suspect
that he intended to accomplish his ambition with Russian assistance, and that, as a result, Russian influence might prevail in
Lhasa before long.[5]

On 3 January 1899 the energetic Lord Curzon became Viceroy of
India. Deeply suspicious of Russian policy, he was determined to
reverse what he regarded as the dilatory and conservative policies

that had hitherto prevailed in London and Calcutta, and to force the British Government to adopt a more determined response to the Russian advances in Central Asia. He could hardly have chosen a more unsuitable time to embark on such a programme. By the end of the year the weak and divided Salisbury administration found itself faced with the costly war in South Africa, which was soon absorbing almost the entire resources of the Empire. Nevertheless, Curzon's persistence was, to some extent, finally rewarded.[6]

He soon began to urge London to set aside the treaties which required that relations with Tibet should be dealt with only through Peking, and to allow him to establish direct relations with the Dalai Lama, thus enabling him to combat Russian intrigues. When the Amir of Afghanistan showed signs of responding to Russia's advances, Curzon pressed the India Office to authorize him to refuse subsidies and arms to the Amir until the latter had entered into more binding assurances of co-operation with India than were provided for under the existing Anglo-Afghan treaty. As for the Persian Gulf, he clamoured for a strong declaration by the British Government that England would resist the incursions of foreign powers, and for the strengthening of British relations with local rulers, and even the seizure of a Gulf port if necessary. He advocated an Anglo-Indian loan to Persia as a means of restoring British influence there, and he was supported by Sir Arthur Hardinge, the British Minister in Tehran, who warned his superiors that unless England was prepared to lend money to the Persians on inadequate security, Persia would become a Russian dependency.

The British Government turned a deaf ear to his appeals. England was in no position to embark on such a costly scheme, which, furthermore, might lead to hostilities with both France and Russia. Curzon railed against the defeatist attitude of the Home Government, which seemed to him to be incapable of formulating a coherent Central Asian and Persian policy. As Lord George Hamilton, the Indian Secretary, remarked gloomily in December 1901, 'the forces in the North behind Russia, military, diplomatic and financial, are on the wax, ours are on the wane'.[7]

Nevertheless, a combination of Curzon's relentless pressure, growing alarm in London about the seeming magnitude of the Russian threat in Central Asia, Lansdowne's more determined policy, and the improved situation in South Africa after 1900, did lead to some counter measures. These, while inadequate by Curzon's standards, improved the situation in England's favour. Thus Lansdowne, in January 1902, warned Russia that England would never consent to a Russian naval or military station on the Persian Gulf, and, a year later, made the declaration about British policy in the Gulf already referred to.[8] At the same time he informed the Russians that he could not agree to the despatch of a Russian political agent to Kabul. At the end of 1903 Curzon made a theatrical naval tour of the Persian Gulf, designed to demonstrate to the world British preponderance there.[9] Despite objections from London, Curzon also managed by 1904 to strengthen British ties with the rulers of Mohammerah, Muscat, Bahrein and Kuweit in the Gulf—a considerable achievement in view of Britain's isolation at this time.[10]

The British were also able to register a few gains in Persia. Following a second Russian loan in 1902 England made a small advance to the Persians in 1903. In 1901 an Australian millionaire, William Knox d'Arcy, secured a concession from the Persian Government for oil exploration in practically the whole of Persia—a significant stroke in view of Russia's strong influence in Tehran.[11] Nevertheless, these advances were puny when compared with Russia's seemingly overwhelming position in the country.[12]

In Tibet Curzon was also able to achieve a short-lived success. In 1903 he persuaded the British Government to agree to the despatch of a British Mission to Tibet led by Sir Francis Younghusband. The ostensible purpose of the mission was to meet Tibetan and Chinese delegates to discuss commercial and frontier questions, although in fact Curzon intended that it should assert British political interests in Tibet. Curzon and Younghusband were able to utilize both Tibetan delaying tactics and reports of their military preparations to justify Younghusband's advance on Lhasa, which the Cabinet had initially forbidden for fear of arousing Russian opposition. After some fighting Younghusband reached Lhasa in July 1904. The Dalai Lama fled, and on 7 September 1904 Younghusband induced the Tibetans to sign a treaty which virtually turned Tibet into a British puppet, although it contained no provision for British interference with her internal affairs. Under its terms Tibet promised to have no relations with foreign Powers without British consent, not to alienate Tibetan land to foreigners, to pay England an indemnity of £500,000, to grant India more favourable trading opportunities, to allow occasional visits of a British trade agent to Lhasa, and to accept an occupation of the Chumbi Valley by British forces for seventy-five years. The Cabinet was aghast when it read the severe terms of this treaty, which went beyond anything that it had authorized. Lansdowne had promised Russia that a British protectorate over Tibet would not be established, and fearing complications with Russia, the Cabinet insisted that both the indemnity and the period of occupation be considerably reduced (to three years), and that the clause allowing the trade agent to visit Lhasa be annulled. Curzon left the Government in no doubt as to his views about the changes: his protests were however in vain.[13] To add to his discomfiture the Cabinet, early in 1905, accepted the Amir of Afghanistan's offer to renew his father's treaty with England, despite Curzon's demand for more far-reaching changes in Indo-Afghan relations.[14] He described it as a 'surrender', and commented bitterly that, 'I have known all along that, with a moribund Government with fear of Russia on the brain, there could be no other ending.'[15] In August 1905 Curzon resigned, probably as much in despair about the complacency of London in the face of Russia as about his difficulties with the Commander in Chief of the Indian Army, Lord Kitchener.[16]

The Liberal Administration was faced with the same problems as its predecessor in dealing with Russia's steady penetration of North Persia, and her military threat to India, which showed no signs of diminishing despite her defeat in the Far East. Both Lord Minto (who succeeded Curzon), and Kitchener pressed for a firm stand against further Russian advances in the area. A C.I.D. sub-committee, meeting early in 1907, and attended by Grey, Morley, and Haldane, recommended the spending of a substantial sum on strategic railways to the frontier to counter lines which Russia was building to the Afghan border, and the despatch of 100,000 troops to India in the event of a Russian invasion of Afghanistan.

The Liberals were even more reluctant than the Unionists had been to provide extra money for Indian defence. For this reason Grey received valuable support from Haldane and Morley in his efforts to reach agreement with Russia. 'We have not got the men to spare and that's the plain truth of it,' Morley remarked in 1906.[17] The circumstances were more favourable for an Anglo-Russian accommodation in 1906. Lansdowne and Sir Charles Hardinge had already laid the groundwork for a settlement, while France was, for obvious reasons, keen on it. The new Russian Foreign Minister, Alexander Isvolsky, wanted to improve Russia's relations with other Powers and secure a relaxation of tension in Central Asia, so that Russia could concentrate on the task of internal reconstruction. Hence Nicolson was sent to St Petersburg in May 1906 with instructions from Asquith, Morley, and Grey to work for an agreement with Russia. The negotiations between him and Isvolsky, which began in June, proceeded slowly. Their progress was not assisted by the internal strife in Russia, which culminated in the Tsar's dissolution of the Duma on 22 July 1906, and which in turn provoked strong protests from British Liberals. The negotiations were also delayed by Isvolsky's need to persuade the Russian Army to accept an Anglo-Russian agreement, and, on the British side, by the strenuous objections of Minto and his advisers to a deal with Russia. Minto summed up his opposition to co-operation with Russia in letters to Morley in 1908. The Viceroy doubted that the convention would change in any way

> the procedure Russia has for years followed in Central Asia and on the frontier of Afghanistan . . . I have never liked the price we are paying for Russia's goodwill, i.e. the obligation to be hand in glove with the most autocratic, cruel and corrupt of powers— neither, I think, can it be very acceptable to you![18]

However, Morley and Grey, in their anxiety to complete negotiations with Russia, ignored the views of the Government of India. Isvolsky, on the other hand, could not so easily over-ride the views of the Russian army leaders. Thus, although Nicolson and Isvolsky had, by April 1907, reached agreement on Persia and Central Asia, the Russian Foreign Minister announced that he could not authorize signature since the military were still criticizing the arrangement. Nicolson and Grey therefore suggested a possible British concession—an offer to discuss an alteration in the rule of the Straits in Russia's favour. The British, of course, had long since abandoned any idea of forcing the Straits by themselves,[19] although they had, during the Russo-Japanese war, warned Russia that any attempt by her Black Sea fleet to enter the Mediterranean would be regarded as a *casus belli*. Grey was not certain what kind of concession England should make and he left it to Isvolsky to formulate suggestions. Later, however, Grey became uneasy about the possible reaction of British public opinion to any change in the rule of the Straits, and he therefore asked Isvolsky to defer further consideration of the question until a later date. Nevertheless, the suggestion had done its work—the Convention was signed on 31 August 1907.

It consisted of three sections. Persia was divided into three zones. Although the two countries promised to respect Persian independence, and to uphold the open door, England undertook not to interfere in, or attempt to secure concessions in the North, which became Russia's sphere of influence, while Russia made similar pledges in respect of a smaller area in the south-east, which became the British sphere. The rest of the country was to be a neutral zone, open to the commerce of both powers. England guaranteed not to alter the political status quo in Afghanistan and pledged that she would not encourage the Amir to adopt measures likely to threaten Russia. For her part Russia accepted that Afghanistan was in England's sphere of influence. Both countries recognized the territorial integrity of Tibet and promised not to interfere with its internal administration. England could continue her existing commercial relations with Tibet, but all other negotiations were to be conducted through the intermediary of the Chinese Government. Britain agreed to hasten the withdrawal of her troops from the Chumbi Valley. Also incorporated in the agreement was a separate declaration by Grey that the British Government intended to preserve the status quo in the Gulf and maintain British trading rights there.[20]

Grey, Morley, and Haldane were satisfied that the Convention would put an end to the long and expensive friction between the two countries in Central Asia, while the Foreign Office hoped that it would lead to Anglo-Russian co-operation against Germany in Europe. The Entente with Russia was not popular in England, and it steadily became more unpopular as the years went by. A small group of Unionists, led by Curzon, attacked the Convention on the grounds that it gave too much to Russia, too little to England. A rather more substantial number of Liberals and radicals regarded the prospect of co-operation with reactionary

Russia with intense distaste. While France was often criticized in radical circles, the Entente with her was far more acceptable to them than that with Russia. To most Liberals Russia was an alien land, backward and reactionary. Her ill-treatment of Jews and other minorities was regarded with particular loathing.[21] Nor was the Indian Government ever fully reconciled to the agreement, and it continued to believe that Russia entertained expansionist designs in Central Asia. Her activities in Persia before 1914 provided India with some evidence for its suspicions. Indeed, given the strength of the opposition to the Convention, particularly in his own party, Grey displayed considerable skill in maintaining it all in the years down to 1914.

Aftermath: Anglo-Russian Relations and Persia

Persia provided Grey's critics with much of their ammunition with which to attack the Entente. Russia's actions there rendered Grey's position exceedingly difficult at times. Hardinge admitted on one occasion that 'we have to suppress the truth and resort to subterfuge at times to meet hostile public opinion'.[22] The Convention merely papered over the difference in the outlook of the two countries towards Persia.[23] In these years the country was convulsed by a struggle between the Nationalists and the Shah. Inevitably Russia favoured an autocratic régime in Persia, which would forward her interests in the North. Grey, conscious of radical pressures, was sympathetic to the Nationalist cause. In any case, at least at first, he genuinely believed that a constitutional régime offered the country greater opportunity for regeneration than a reactionary one. At the same time the anti-Russian constitutionalists tended to look to England for support. Not that they ever received much beyond vague expressions of sympathy, even in the years before 1907. England had no wish to promote revolution in Persia. Although Grey was initially optimistic that the Russians might support him in encouraging Persia's efforts to reform herself, he soon became disillusioned, not only with Russia, but with the Persian Nationalists as well.

His officials never had any faith in the Persian Nationalists. Like Grey, they believed that the Russian Entente was essential to British security in Europe, and they were not prepared to jeopardize it for the sake of Persia. Nicolson summed up the

Foreign Office attitude in August 1911: 'The maintenance, both in letter and spirit, of the Convention is of far more importance than the . . . position of Persia . . . The Persians are perfectly hopeless . . . The Mejliss [Parliament] has done nothing and things are worse than before.'[24] Nevertheless, Russia's actions in Persia frequently strained the agreement almost to breaking-point as Grey, in a sense morally committed to the constitutionalists, and anxious about Liberal opinion at home, felt bound to try to curb the worst excesses of the Russians.

Persia's administration had long been racked by inefficiency and corruption. The Shah, Mozaffer ed Din, was a worthless creature who relied on Russian subsidies to enable him to maintain a luxurious style of living. He entirely ignored the welfare of his subjects. The Shah's neglect of his country, and his evident willingness to allow the resources of Northern Persia to fall increasingly into Russian hands, provoked a growing internal agitation against his régime towards the end of the nineteenth century. The unrest was fanned by the large loans he contracted with the Russian Government in 1900 and 1902. Indeed, after 1900 Arthur Hardinge gave limited financial assistance from Embassy funds to the more conservative of the Nationalists in the hope that the growing anti-Russian feeling amongst his subjects might force the Shah to reverse his policy. Disorder became more pronounced in 1905, when the Shah secured a further Russian loan, and on 30 July 1906 he was forced to promise a constitution to his subjects, a promise which, after outbreaks of almost revolutionary proportions, he fulfilled on 1 January 1907. Shortly afterwards he died. His successor, Mohammed Ali, was no improvement, and, indeed, while promising to uphold the constitution, he secretly intrigued to overthrow it, and at the same time blocked all reforms proposed by the Mejliss.

The Anglo-Russian Convention was received with disgust by the Persian Nationalists, who exaggerated the amount of support they had received from England. They accused the British of abandoning their cause and of conspiring with Russia to partition their country. In fact the Convention did, to some extent, inhibit Russian activity in Persia—Isvolsky, who had no wish to alienate England at the outset, managed to restrain the Russian army from sending troops to Persia to crush the revolutionaries, and did co-operate with England in December 1907 to press the Shah to abide by the constitution. However, he made little effort to restrain Russian agents in Persia, for on 23 June 1908 the Shah, with the aid of the Russian officered Persian Cossack Brigade, and with the probable approval of the Russian Minister in Persia, closed the Mejliss and suspended the constitution. Isvolsky now wanted Grey to agree to an Anglo-Russian loan, which would enable the Shah to strengthen his hold on his country. Grey rejected the proposal. British radical opinion was already agitated about the recent developments in Persia, and the Cabinet refused to consider a loan until the Shah had restored the constitution. The ensuing deadlock led to mutual recriminations about each other's lack of co-operation in Persia.

The situation became even more tense in the spring and summer of 1909 when Nationalist revolts broke out all over Persia, and which the Shah's feeble forces were quite unable to contain. Russia despatched troops to the North, ostensibly to protect Russian lives and property, although the British suspected that she was meditating intervention on the side of the Shah. The Nationalist forces soon began to converge on Tehran, and Grey protested vehemently at St Petersburg when he learnt that the Russian army was planning to occupy the capital, and thereby save the Shah from the wrath of his subjects. Isvolsky became irritated by Grey's protests and both Hardinge and Nicolson warned the Foreign Secretary that his continued exhortations might endanger the Entente. Although the Cabinet was taking a keen interest in Persian developments, this did not prevent Grey from telegraphing his private assurances to Isvolsky that, even if Russia did occupy Tehran, he need not fear that 'I shall cease to keep in touch or shall regard our relations as in any way less cordial.'[25] Thus Grey was extremely relieved when he learnt that on 16 July the Nationalists had taken Tehran and deposed the Shah, all without Russian interference.

Grey needed some token of Russian goodwill if a projected visit of Nicholas II to Cowes in August 1909 was not to be marred by quarrels over Persia. Nicolson and Hardinge promoted and smoothed the way for this visit, despite the fears of Asquith and Grey that it would provoke hostile demonstrations from their Liberal and radical supporters. In the event the visit passed off successfully and pleased the Tsar, although on the official level it accomplished little, since Grey failed to persuade Isvolsky, who accompanied Nicholas, to agree to evacuate the North of Persia. Now Grey wanted to help the constitutional régime by means of an Anglo-Russian loan, whereas Isvolsky, complaining bitterly about the anti-Russian attitude of the constitutionalists, not only refused a loan, but also rejected Grey's persistent appeals to withdraw Russian troops from the country.

The dispute over Persia dragged on into 1910. In February Isvolsky was cajoled into agreeing to a loan, but he insisted that Persia must accept a number of conditions designed to assert Anglo-Russian predominance in the country and to secure the proper administration of her finances. One of these demands required the Persian Government to employ neutral experts in the Ministry of Finance.

Persia refused to agree to some of the demands. Isvolsky rejected Grey's pleas to grant the loan without any conditions. Grey was growing increasingly anxious about internal developments in Persia. As 1910 progressed the Persian Government, hovering on the verge of bankruptcy, began to lose control of its outlying provinces, in which anarchy and lawlessness thrived. In the South, British trade was seriously affected. To the complaints of the British radicals about British policy in Persia were added those of British traders, who were incurring heavy losses. They too invariably attributed Persia's difficulties to the Russian occupation of the North, which, they claimed, was discrediting the Central Government in the eyes of the people. Grey hoped that part of any Anglo-Russian loan would be used to establish a native gendarmerie in the South, under the control of neutral officers. This force would, he hoped, obviate the need for large-scale British intervention there, a course beyond Indian finances and which, moreover, would only encourage the Russian interventionists in the North.

In the autumn of 1910 there were changes at London and St Petersburg which, Grey hoped, might pave the way for improved Anglo-Russian relations in Persia. Isvolsky was transferred to the Paris Embassy, and his place in the Russian Foreign Ministry taken by his deputy, Sazonov. At the same time Hardinge was appointed as Viceroy of India, where it was expected that he would pay more attention to the susceptibilities of the Russians than had Minto. Nicolson was brought to London to replace him, because, in Grey's words, 'there is no one else personally so fitted to fill the vacancy at the Foreign Office and to preserve that continuity of policy here on which the maintenance of good relations with [the] Russian Government depend'.[26] His appointment was not a success. He had enjoyed his work at St Petersburg and had not wanted to come to London. His health was poor, he was unhappy at the Foreign Office, and on several occasions he asked Grey if he could be posted abroad. He took less account than had Hardinge of Grey's Parliamentary and Cabinet difficulties, and, a keen advocate of the Russian connection, he was always pressing Grey to turn the Ententes into alliances, despite the obvious impossibility of such a course.

The advent of Sazonov brought no alleviation of Britain's difficulties in Persia. Like Isvolsky, he supported the Entente, but believed that England needed Russian co-operation so much in Europe that she would be prepared to ignore Russian advances in Persia. He refused to lend money to the Persians, and soon began to put forward demands on the Persian Government for further concessions in the North, and, despite Grey's protests, threatened to use force to secure Persian compliance. Nicolson remained throughout concerned that the Entente might collapse, and, in its interest, he would have preferred Grey to overlook Russia's actions in Persia. He wrote to the *Chargé* at St Petersburg, shortly after taking up his post that:

> It is . . . of vital importance that our harmonious relations should not be disturbed, and the little breezes which sometimes arise ought not to upset either the Russian equanimity or our own . . . I look upon our understanding with Russia, as well as . . . with France, as the bedrock of our foreign policy.[27]

However, after January 1911 there was a welcome lull in the tension when the Russians agreed to a loan and to the withdrawal of their troops from the North, which took place in April. Grey was able to persuade the Persians to set up a Swedish-led gendarmerie. A beginning was made by the Mejliss with its reorganization, under neutral experts, of the antiquated and venal Persian administration, when an American, W. Morgan Shuster, was appointed Treasurer-general in the Persian Ministry of Finance.

The relief was purely temporary. It was not long before the reforming zeal of the American came into conflict with Russia's determination to brook no interference in her sphere of influence in the North. Shuster, anxious not to offend his new employers, somewhat tactlessly failed to consult the Russians before attempting to place the revenues of the North more firmly under his control. He occasioned them serious anguish by appointing an anti-Russian British Indian Army Officer, Major Charles Stokes, to organize a Treasury gendarmerie, whose task was to superintend the collection of taxes in the whole of Persia. The British were, for their part, considerably upset when the ex-Shah, who had been exiled from Persia after his fall, returned to the North in July in a bid to recover his throne. The Foreign Office believed (correctly) that the Russians had connived at his return, and they were confirmed in this view when Neratov, who took over the Russian Foreign Ministry during Sazanov's long illness in 1911, refused to agree not to recognize the ex-Shah if he succeeded in his aim, and proposed that the two countries should remain neutral in the struggle.[28]

Neratov called for the dismissal of Stokes and threatened to reoccupy the North if the Persian Government did not give way. Grey, anxious to retain Russian goodwill during the Moroccan crisis, and yet conscious of radical opinion at home, eventually agreed, on 17 May, that Stokes should not be employed in the North, and to suspend India Office authority for his secondment from the Indian Army. These moves did not satisfy the Russians, who demanded that Stokes should leave Persia altogether. Grey continued to attempt to find some compromise, but without success. He soon upset Shuster, who began to publish indictments in the British press of Anglo-Russian policy in Persia, and even to propose more British subjects for service in the North. Nor would the Persian Government save Grey's face by dismissing Stokes.

Matters came to a head at the end of October when, after a clash between Shuster's gendarmerie and some Russian-led Persian Cossacks, Neratov despatched Russian troops to the North and threatened not to withdraw them until Shuster had been dismissed. Grey begged the Russians not to alienate British opinion by occupying Tehran, while at the same time he urged the Persian Government to comply with the Russian demand. The Persians refused. During November and December matters became even more serious when, after despatching reinforcements to the North, the Russian Government presented Persia with a series of peremptory ultimata threatening the immediate occupation of Tehran if Shuster was not dismissed, and new demands accepted which would further increase Russia's hold on the North. On 2 December Grey warned Benckendorff that if Russia took further action he would have to resign and denounce the Convention in public speeches. He was being sorely pressed by his radical critics.

However, the situation was saved in the nick of time, partly as a result of an appeal by Grey to Sazonov, who had recovered from his illness and was on a visit to Paris, to return to St Petersburg quickly and save the Entente. On 9 December Neratov told Buchanan that Russian troops would be held at Kazvin and would be recalled if Russia's demands were accepted. On 22 December the Persian Government capitulated—Shuster left Persia on 11 January 1912, while Stokes had already been recalled by the India Office.

Russia's victory marked the beginning of a new stage in Persia's troubles. The Russians, despite their promises, failed to remove their troops from the North, and Grey decided not to upset them by further pressure. He wrote in January 1912 that 'if the Agreement were to go, everything would be worse both for us and Persia. So I stake everything upon pulling the Agreement through all difficulties.'[29]

Relations between the two countries remained stormy throughout 1912. Russian reinforcements were still being sent to the North, where Russian consuls were behaving like rulers. They continued to encourage the cause of the ex-Shah, despite a promise by Sazonov to facilitate his retirement from the country.[30] In April 1912 Russian troops bombarded a Moslem shrine in Meshed. Grey was 'disgusted'[31] and he warned Sazonov that the incident had upset Moslem opinion in the British Empire. His continued exhortations upset Sazonov who complained that 'Russian public opinion would be estranged, did it become known that its Government was being lectured at like a child at every step which it took to safeguard its interests.'[32] Nicolson entirely agreed with the Russian Foreign Minister 'that he is occasionally spoken to in a schoolmasterly fashion' and promised to try to moderate the tone of future British representations. 'The long and short of it is that we are on exceedingly good relations with Russia and must do our best to continue these relations.'[33] During the summer conditions in Persia went from bad to worse. There were continuous cabinet crises in Tehran, and even Grey now began to talk of allowing the ex-Shah to return to his throne if he could do so without seeming to rely on Russian support.

The Foreign Office was now becoming receptive to Russian hints that the Convention might be revised to give Russia a freer hand in the North, while Nicolson meditated a British occupation of the South and the extension of her influence into the neutral zone. Crewe, Secretary of State for India after 1910, commented that 'it is a poor outcome of the Convention, if things so end, because it is apparently identical with what would have happened if there had been no Convention.'[34]

At the same time Hardinge was becoming alarmed by increasing Russian activity in the outer provinces of China, chiefly in Outer Mongolia and in Chinese Turkestan (Sinkiang). The Chinese Revolution of 1911 weakened China's hold over these provinces and, as a result, in December 1911, Outer Mongolia declared her independence of China, and appealed to Russia for recognition and support. In June 1912 Russia increased her consular guard at Kashgar, the capital of Sinkiang. She claimed that this was necessitated by increasing disorders in the town, but the Indian Government feared that Russia might soon declare a protectorate over the whole province.

England had neither the means nor the desire to do more than make anxious enquiries at St Petersburg about her policy in Chinese Central Asia. Nevertheless, Hardinge believed that England had a right to compensation for these changes in the Central Asian status quo. He therefore contemplated a return to the Curzonian policy of bringing Tibet into closer relations with India.

In February 1910 a Chinese army entered Lhasa and restored full Chinese sovereignty. The Dalai Lama fled to India. The British, faithful to the policy of non-intervention, refused to help him to regain his temporal power. In 1911 the Chinese garrison in Lhasa mutinied, and the Tibetans took advantage of the ensuing confusion to besiege the Chinese troops in the capital. Hardinge anticipated that the Dalai Lama would soon return to his country and he feared that the Tibetan ruler, despairing of British assistance, might again appeal to Russia for help in expelling the Chinese from Tibetan soil.

The British Government would not allow the Viceroy to offer Indian military assistance to the Dalai Lama. Hardinge initiated an alternative method of aiding the Tibetan ruler, which, he hoped, would be acceptable to London—a mission by a British Indian police official, Laden La, to Lhasa to arrange a ceasefire between the Tibetans and the Chinese, and to secure the evacuation of the Chinese garrison. Hardinge hoped that the Dalai Lama would then return to his country full of gratitude for India's action, while Laden La might remain permanently in Lhasa. Even this device was, however, too much for the British Government. Morley and Grey led the Cabinet in ordering Hardinge to recall Laden La. Grey feared that Hardinge's initiative would upset Russia. Eventually the Chinese garrison was repatriated to China via India, and the Dalai returned to his capital. Hardinge was still dissatisfied. He remained anxious in case the Dalai Lama turned to Russia for support against China, and he pressed Crewe and Grey to secure Russian agreement to the appointment of a British resident in Lhasa who would keep an eye on the Dalai. In return Hardinge suggested that England offer to agree to an increase in Russian influence in Kashgar and Outer Mongolia.[35]

In September 1912 Sazonov visited England to discuss the deteriorating situation in Persia, and Grey's critics feared that the partition of Persia was now imminent. Protests poured into the Foreign Office and Grey complained that he was being 'bombarded with letters from people here who want me to break with Russia over Persia; how on earth can we help Persia if we do?' He reaffirmed that 'partition . . . is not yet in question and I trust may never be.'[36] There were preparatory talks between Crewe, Morley, Grey, and Asquith. Crewe persuaded the Ministers to oppose the restoration of the ex-Shah on the grounds that the Government would look 'such utter fools that the step should be avoided at almost any cost'.[37]

Sazonov had talks with Grey at Balmoral between 24 and 27 September. He agreed not to partition Persia, nor to allow the ex-Shah to recover his throne. However, Grey approved the appointment of the pro-Russian Sa'd ud-Dowla as Regent of Persia, the previous Regent having fled to Europe in the summer in despair at the confusion and anarchy prevailing in the country. Sazonov believed that the new Regent would install a government in Tehran which would favour Russia's interests in the

North. Grey for his part hoped for renewed Anglo-Russian co-operation to support the Central Government, and Russian participation in a large joint loan to promote Persia's recovery. Grey mentioned to Sazonov the possibility of setting up British-officered road guards to patrol the South and the neutral zone, since the Swedish-led gendarmerie was not fulfilling British expectations. He also suggested that Sazonov agree to closer Anglo-Tibetan relations. Neither proposal was much favoured by the Russian Foreign Minister unless Russia secured substantial concessions elsewhere: he claimed that Russia had no intention of altering the status either of Outer Mongolia or Sinkiang. Hardinge's hope for a Tibet-Central Asian deal was therefore frustrated. Sazonov demanded a freer hand for Russia in North Persia, and suggested the division of the neutral sphere between the two countries: Grey made no comment on the first and deprecated the second of these two suggestions.

Sazonov seemed pleased by the visit, although little that was constructive emerged from it. Things in Persia were evidently to go on much as before. Grey commented: 'I am not under the illusion that we have solved the Persian difficulty. Sazonov is too sanguine.'[38]

Between 1909 and 1912 Russia, bitterly antagonistic towards the Nationalist Government at Tehran, concentrated on pursuing her interest in North Persia, and paid little heed to Grey's frequent protests. Grey hoped that Russia would co-operate with England to uphold the authority of the Central Government: the Russians, however, were not interested in bolstering up a Government which was so hostile to their interests. Russia would only uphold a régime, such as that of the ex-Shah, which was prepared to become virtually a Russian puppet. Russia's policy in Persia excited vociferous criticisms of the Entente from British radicals, and made Grey's position increasingly difficult. Nevertheless, Grey could justify the maintenance of the Convention. He pointed out that while, on the one hand, the radicals demanded a limited and pacific foreign policy, on the other, they called for whole-hearted support for the independence of Persia. These two demands could not be reconciled. The 1907 Convention affirmed Russia's preponderance in the North, a preponderance England had been unable to challenge effectively in the years of hostility prior to 1907. The agreement had also enabled the British Government to stabilize the size of the Indian army. Grey believed that if England broke with Russia over Persia, the pre-1907 antagonism in Central Asia would reappear and as a result British forces in India would have to be considerably reinforced. Such measures would provoke an outcry from the radicals who were already demanding reduced service estimates. He claimed that the very existence of the Convention enabled him to restrain Russia from behaving even more imperiously in Persia, although he too became angry at times when his appeals were repeatedly ignored.

His arguments seem to have been accepted even by those British Ministers who took a close interest in Persian affairs for, despite the campaign against the Entente in the country, there is no evidence that there was ever a Ministerial revolt against his Persian policy. Harcourt was rumoured in 1909 to be leading a Cabinet cabal against the Convention with Russia, and in September 1912 he protested about reports that Grey and Sazonov intended to partition the country. But Grey was also reluctant to contemplate partition, which would increase the already over-taxed resources of the British Empire. Lord Loreburn, one of Grey's most virulent critics in these years, refused to protest about his Persian policy. He told C. P. Scott at the end of 1911 that he regarded Persia as a 'red herring', distracting public opinion from Anglo-German relations, and described the Persians as a corrupt and hopeless race, the Mejliss as 'absurd and incompetent', and Shuster as a 'pushing American'.[39] Although Lloyd George argued in 1912 that an Anglo-German agreement would give England Germany's diplomatic support in Persia, he failed to explain what good this would be against Russia's massive presence in the area, and her absolute determination not to be dislodged from it.

Given the attitude of the Cabinet, Grey was able to continue his policy of maintaining the Anglo-Russian Entente, partly as a brake on Russia's ambitions in Persia, but also as a reinsurance against German aggression in Europe. Nevertheless, the situation in Persia became even more chaotic after 1912, and it was not a good advertisement for Grey's policy.

England and Turkey

British influence in Turkey continued to decline after 1897 while that of Germany correspondingly increased.[40] Nor was England's position in Constantinople in any way enhanced by her efforts to promote the introduction of reforms in strife-torn Macedonia.[41] The Macedonians had, in 1893, set up the Internal Macedonian Revolutionary Organization to work for the creation of an autonomous Macedonia. Bulgaria encouraged the movement in the expectation that, if Turkish rule in Europe collapsed, she would inherit Macedonia. Soon bands of Bulgarian and Macedonian terrorists infiltrated the province in order to rally the populace against Turkey. They perpetrated a series of outrages in Macedonia—assassinations, attacks on public buildings and other facilities, etc.—in order to provoke the Turkish army into reprisals, exaggerated accounts of which were published in the European presses. By keeping the agitation in Macedonia alive, the bands hoped that they would provoke Great Power intervention to force the Turks to grant autonomy to the province.

These often Bulgarian-inspired activities alerted the other Balkan states to the danger that Macedonia, if it became autonomous, might drift into the arms of Bulgaria. They were determined that they too should have a share in any future partition of Macedonia. Thus after 1903 Serbian and Greek organized and subsidized bands began to appear in Macedonia, seeking to eradicate Bulgarian influence from as large an area of the province as possible and substitute for it Greek or Serbian influence. Macedonia became the scene of a vicious internecine racial struggle for the ultimate control of the country, with the Turks often reduced to the role of not unwilling spectators of a war of extermination amongst her Christian subjects.

Inevitably the Powers had to intervene, if only to prevent war between Bulgaria and Turkey, which might involve one or other of the Great Powers. The British were the prime movers for reforms in the province. Tales of Turkish atrocities soon awakened the English nonconformist and humanitarian conscience, and in 1903 a Balkan Committee was set up in London, composed of Liberals, Church leaders and numerous other worthies, to exert vigorous pressure on the Government to work for reforms in Macedonia. Britain's room for manoeuvre was, however, limited.

Austria and Russia had ended their rivalry in the Balkans in 1897 by reaching agreement to preserve the status quo in the Peninsula. Consequently, these two countries insisted on taking the lead in proposing reforms at Constantinople. As they had no desire to weaken the Sultan's authority in any appreciable degree, since this would endanger the stability of Turkey-in-Europe, their proposals were inevitably of a limited nature. Germany, anxious to retain her influence in Turkey, also acted as a drag on reform proposals, while France, mindful of her huge investments in the country, and anxious to keep in step with her Russian ally, likewise did little. In these circumstances, the Sultan, Abdul Hamid, was able to frustrate and delay the application of reforms in Macedonia, and severely limit European surveillance of the reforms, which, he judged (rightly as it turned out) would be fatal to his authority and prestige in the Empire.[42]

Consequently Lansdowne was unable to accomplish much in the way of reform up to 1905. When the bands promoted an uprising in October 1902, which was ruthlessly crushed by the Turks, he was able to pressurize Austria and Russia into formulating the so-called Vienna scheme of reforms, which proposed the reorganization of the Macedonian gendarmerie, revenue, and taxation systems, with the help of European advisers. The Turks did nothing in 1903 and the situation in Macedonia became even more chaotic. In the autumn there was a further uprising, which convinced Lansdowne that something more drastic was required. He suggested that an autonomous Macedonia was the only answer to the problem; but the Austrians and Russians rejected such a far-reaching suggestion, and would only agree to a new programme of reforms in October, which included the appointment of two European civil agents to assist the Turkish Inspector-General of the province, of European officers to reorganize the gendarmerie, and numerous administrative and judicial reforms. Apart from the appointment of a few European gendarmerie officers in 1904, Turkish obstruction was sufficient to render abortive the bulk of this programme. The Turks blamed the activities of the rival bands for impeding the progress of the reforms, and, accordingly, Greece, Bulgaria, and Serbia were deluged with appeals from the Powers during the next few years to abandon their encouragement of the bands; appeals which, for the most part, fell on deaf ears.

In 1905 Austria and Russia went a little further towards satisfying Lansdowne's pleas that all reforms would be still-born unless there was a greater degree of European supervision. They proposed the establishment of an international commission in Macedonia, which was to supervise the reorganization of the provincial revenues. The Powers argued that an increase in these revenues would enable the Turks to press ahead more strenuously with the other reforms. The Turks, however, baulked at the appointment of Europeans to the commission, and they were only brought to agree, in November 1905, by a half-hearted international naval demonstration off Mitylene, which Lansdowne had proposed, and from which Germany stood ostentatiously apart.

The disorders in Macedonia worsened in 1906. Grey, now Foreign Secretary, concentrated on trying to put the existing reform programme into operation. He was somewhat dubious that much could be done in view of Turkey's implacable hostility, the continued activities of the bands in Macedonia, and the refusal of the other Powers to go very far in coercing the Turks. The Balkan Committee was extremely critical of what they described as his dilatory policy, while Grey himself, fortified by a large Liberal majority in Parliament, at first paid considerably less attention to their strictures than had Lansdowne.[43]

By 1907, however, oppressed by the mounting anarchy in Macedonia, Grey adopted a more determined line. He now proposed that the bulk of the Turkish army should be withdrawn from Macedonia, and replaced by an expanded European-led gendarmerie. This, he considered, would be a more economical and efficient method of restoring order than the use of troops. The Sultan feared that this plan would place his province almost entirely in European hands, while the Powers, by 1908, had, in any case, lost interest in the futile reform agitation. Consequently, Grey threatened to withdraw altogether from the feeble Concert, and to inform his parliamentary critics that the blame for the failure of Macedonian reforms lay with the other European Powers.

The Anglo-Russian Convention did not result in more fervent Russian support for the reform programme. Contrary to the hopes of the Foreign Office, Isvolsky had no intention of allowing the Convention to stand in the way of good relations with Germany, or of continued Austro-Russian co-operation in the Balkans.[44] However, the Sultan's award of a railway concession in Macedonia to Austria in February 1908 altered the situation, to some extent, in England's favour. Isvolsky was convinced that the concession foreshadowed the renewal by Austria of her strategic and economic penetration of the Balkans, and decided that, as a result, the 1897 agreement had collapsed. He was correspondingly more willing to co-operate with England in the Balkans. England believed that Aehrenthal, the Austrian Foreign Minister, had secured the concession from the Sultan in return for a promise that he would impede the further progress of reforms.

Grey and his officials were even more delighted when, towards the end of 1907, Germany irritated both England and Russia by attempting to secure banking and other concessions in Tehran. Hardinge rejoiced that 'Germany is driving Russia into our arms', and he hoped that if England played 'the game quite straightly with Russia in Persia . . . we ought to have her entirely with us, not only in Asia, but in Europe also.'[45] England and Russia were soon discussing a joint programme of reforms for Macedonia. Final details were drawn up by Hardinge and Isvolsky during the course of a visit by the King to meet the Russian Emperor at Reval in June 1908. The German Emperor and the German press complained that England was now trying to encircle Germany with a ring of hostile powers. These complaints were not taken seriously by the Foreign Office. Mallet minuted that:

> so long as France, Russia and England hold together, Germany will not attack. It is a remarkable achievement on the part of Germany to have united against her Englishmen, Slav and Frenchmen in the space of a very few years.[46]

Grey and his officials could well afford to be complacent about Britain's international position in the summer of 1908. Russia appeared to be moving closer to England, while Anglo-Austrian relations improved for a time after the King met Francis Joseph at Ischl in June 1908. The British were very elated by the Young Turk Revolution in Macedonia, which forced the Sultan, on 24 July 1908, to restore the 1876 constitution, and to order elections for a Chamber of Deputies. The movement, which was tenuously controlled by a Committee of Union and Progress, had grown up in the 1880s, and was particularly strong amongst intellectuals and the younger army officers. It was dedicated to reforming the ramshackle Ottoman administration before the Empire collapsed, and was divided amongst the Great Powers. By 1908 the movement was particularly strong in the Turkish army in Macedonia, where the revolt first started. Ironically, the Anglo-Russian agreement and the prospect of a more elaborate system of reforms, with increased European control, provided part of the motive for the revolution. The Committee was composed of two wings, one Liberal and the other Nationalist. The Liberal element was in the ascendant in July 1908 and held out the promise of sweeping reforms and administrative decentralization for the entire Empire. The various nationalities in Macedonia were temporarily reconciled with the new régime, and the disorders in the province subsided.[47] England and Russia accordingly abandoned their joint reform scheme on 27 July.

Even more pleasing from the British point of view was the fact that the Young Turks turned to Britain for advice and assistance, and the Germans, committed as they had been to the Sultan, lost their influence at Constantinople. Grey was soon writing enthusiastic letters to the newly appointed Ambassador at Constantinople, Sir Gerard Lowther, pressing him to support and encourage the Turkish reformers for 'the effects upon the politics of Europe of a strong and reformed Turkey would be very great.'[48]

The Bosnian Crisis

Satisfaction in London at the turn of events was short-lived. As Hardinge had surmised in July, Isvolsky was not very keen on a Liberal Turkey, and both he and Aehrenthal met at Buchlau in Austria in September to discuss how they could take advantage of the changed situation in Turkey. There they drew up a scheme whereby Austria was to annex Bosnia and Herzegovina, the two Turkish provinces which she had occupied in 1878 while Russia, for her part, was to secure changes in her favour in the régime of the Straits. Aehrenthal suddenly announced the annexation of Bosnia and Herzegovina early in October, while Isvolsky was in Paris canvassing French support for the proposed changes at the Straits. At the same time Bulgaria declared her independence of Turkey.[49]

These events caused much anguish in London. They appeared to deal a severe blow to the prestige of the new Turkish régime. Turkey inevitably looked to England to help her to rectify these violations of the Treaty of Berlin. While Grey ruled out the use of force as a means of exerting pressure on Austria and Bulgaria, he recognized that Britain must try to secure for Turkey some financial compensation from the two Powers. He wrote to Asquith on 5 October that, 'I propose that we should be the Turks' friend in the contest: inclination and policy both point that way, for the Young Turk régime is the injured and deserving party.'[50] He used Britain's right as a signatory of the Treaty of Berlin of 1878 to refuse to recognize the Austro-Bulgarian actions until they offered Turkey some restitution, and until the whole affair had been placed on a more legal footing. Indeed, he adopted a highly moral, indignant and querulous tone towards Austria, which caused great irritation in Vienna.

The British had little sympathy for Isvolsky's discomfiture, since they suspected that the Russian Foreign Minister had engaged in some intrigue with Aehrenthal which had redounded to the former's discredit. On the other hand, they recognized that their failure to help him to escape from the consequences of his folly might lead to his fall from office and the collapse of the Entente. Grey found it difficult to hit on a solution that would satisfy both Russia and Turkey. Eventually he decided to accept a Russo-French proposal to call a conference of the Treaty Powers to discuss the question. He had feared originally that a conference would only make the situation worse—with other Powers calling for compensation at Turkey's expense, and much jealousy and friction thereby created. However, when a much chastened Isvolsky arrived in London on 9 October 1908, Grey had no difficulty in persuading him to accept the restriction of the agenda of the conference to the question of financial compensation for Turkey. The Russian Foreign Minister still hoped for some rectification of the Straits régime to restore his tarnished prestige in St Petersburg. Although Grey was prepared to support this demand, the Cabinet, fearing a public outcry, at first overruled him. However, on 14 October, Grey, after further pleas from Isvolsky and in a sense committed by his promises in 1907, returned to the Cabinet with a compromise proposal whereby all nations were to have the right of ingress and egress in wartime, while the Black Sea states alone could exercise this right in peace-time. The Cabinet agreed to this suggestion, although Grey persuaded Isvolsky to defer an approach to Turkey and the other Powers until the Bosnian crisis had been settled. With that Isvolsky departed for Russia seemingly quite satisfied, although he had not impressed any of the British Ministers he had met in London either with his ability or with his straight-forwardness.

The dispute between Austria and Turkey and between Bulgaria and Turkey dragged on throughout the winter. Grey eventually abandoned the idea of a conference in favour of bilateral negotiations between the parties concerned. Neither Bulgaria nor Austria were at first prepared to pay monetary compensation to Turkey, and several times during the winter there were minor crises as rumours circulated of a possible Austro-Bulgarian attack upon Turkey. In November Grey rejected a Turkish proposal for an Anglo-Turkish alliance. He did not want to encourage Turkish obstinacy, nor would the Cabinet have agreed to it, but he recognized that if Austria and Bulgaria did attack Turkey, England's prestige in the Middle East would demand that she should come to the assistance of the Turks.[51] However, this aspect of the crisis receded in the early months of 1909 as first Austria, and then Bulgaria (encouraged by Russian financial assistance), agreed to a monetary settlement of their respective disputes with Turkey. Turkey had wanted territorial compensation from Bulgaria and made difficulties about accepting financial concessions from her. However, Grey warned her that England would not come to her assistance if she became involved in a war with Bulgaria on this issue, and Turkey climbed down.

The crisis was made worse by Isvolsky's decision to champion the claims of Serbia for compensation because of Austria's alteration of the Balkan status quo. While the British had little sympathy for Serbia—Hardinge complained bitterly about 'that wretched little Servia who I fear is bent on mischief unless she can get some territorial compensation for the loss of her national aspirations',[52]—Grey felt bound to offer her some support in order not to displease Russia. The difficulty was that Aehrenthal steadfastly refused to consider ceding Austrian land to Serbia, while Grey would not allow Turkey to be further despoiled. He hoped at first that Germany would assist him in persuading Aehrenthal to change his mind, but the Germans consistently supported their ally throughout the crisis. Grey's dilemma was that the Cabinet, on 24 February 1909, made it clear that war should be avoided over these Balkan issues, whereas Grey realized that, if Austria issued an ultimatum to Serbia to withdraw her claims, Russia and then Germany might be dragged into the ensuing war. He had already, in November 1908, refused to commit himself when Benckendorff had requested him for information as to England's attitude if Russia became involved in a war with Austria and Germany. In order to avoid such a contingency, Grey, in February and March, 1909, steadily abandoned Serbia's claims, while making a show of support for her in order not to irritate Russia.

The problem was eventually resolved on 22 March 1909, when Germany presented her famous 'ultimatum' to Russia demanding Russian recognition of the annexation of Bosnia and Herzegovina without further equivocation, and intimating that war might break out if she refused. Isvolsky had already decided to abandon his support for Serbia's territorial demands, much to Grey's relief. Now Isvolsky, who had hoped that Serbia might obtain, at the very least, economic concessions from Austria, gave way altogether and accepted the annexation for, as he told Nicolson, Russia was still weak, France could not be relied upon, and England would offer only diplomatic assistance.

Although the Foreign Office complained bitterly about Isvolsky's capitulation, it was privately admitted in London that it had enabled England to escape from an increasingly embarrassing situation. Although Grey paraded a final show of determination, and refused a German request, on 25 March, to recognize the annexation, the issue was a foregone conclusion. By the end of March, Grey had followed the Russian example. As Hardinge put it to the King, 'it might be a climb-down' but it had 'the advantage of showing to the whole world that we are ready to stretch a great many points to secure European peace.'[53]

The Central Powers had secured a diplomatic victory at the expense of the Triple Entente. Nevertheless, Grey had steered a course which had led to pecuniary compensation for Turkey, in the face of a Cabinet and country which became increasingly bored by the dispute and which would certainly have opposed a war over questions that seemed remote from British interests. As Grey recognized, England had nothing to offer the various disputants 'except advice, which is equivalent to suggesting a settlement at the expense of other people, who are not prepared to make sacrifices or dare not to face their own people if they do'.[54] Some members of the Cabinet, like Churchill, felt that Grey had over-reacted to Austria's annexation of provinces, which she had occupied for so long and that, as a result, England had been forced to take a leading part in the dispute. Grey's actions in the next Balkan crisis suggest that he had taken the lesson to heart.

Few in London cared about the fate of a 'wretched lot like the Servians',[55] although many officials were concerned about the strained relations between Austria and England which ensued as a result of Grey's intervention. Grey himself took a long time to forgive Austria—'D'Aehrenthal,' he wrote in January 1909, 'is not only unscrupulous himself, but so mean that he never can believe he has honest men to deal with anywhere.'[56] Relations between the two countries remained cool down to 1914.[57] The Foreign Office was also seriously anxious about the effects of the long drawn-out crisis on the relations between England and her Entente partners, and with Turkey.

Anglo-Turkish relations were certainly less close in April 1909 than they had been during the halcyon days of the revolution. The Turks complained of the lukewarm help they had received from England during the crisis,[58] and the meagre gains they had secured as a result of following British advice. Lowther became increasingly despondent about the prospects for the Young Turk régime as the months went by. During the winter time he reported that the anti-British reactionaries were slipping back into power in Constantinople, and that instability and corruption alike were increasing. He anticipated that the end result would be a pro-German military dictatorship. His pessimism increasingly lost him the confidence of his superiors in London. He incurred the resentment of the Turks when he tried to persuade them to accept unpalatable advice, yet, on the other hand, his failure to retain Turkish goodwill earned him the obloquys of Hardinge, Mallet and the others. He was especially attacked for his failure to promote a Turco-Bulgarian Entente, which Hardinge had projected as a possible defensive combination against Austria in the Balkans. Grey and Hardinge remained optimistic about the future of Turkey, especially after the failure of a counter-revolution by

Abdul Hamid in April 1909, which resulted in the abdication of the Sultan. Lowther, on the other hand, found the incident 'nauseating' and commented that, 'all this leads me to the conclusion that reform is out of the question for this wretched country.'[59]

Nor did the Triple Entente emerge from the crisis with that degree of solidarity which the Foreign Office regarded as essential if future Austro-German attempts to assert their predominance in Europe were to be successfully resisted. France showed herself even more reluctant than Britain to support Serbia's claims, while her financiers were co-operating with their German counterparts both in Morocco and in Constantinople. Even more serious from the British point of view was that the Entente with Russia was under great stress. Nicolson feared that Russia would blame her humiliation at the hands of Germany on the ineffectiveness of British support. He pressed his superiors to agree to an alliance with Russia as the only means of saving Isvolsky from dismissal, and his replacement by a reactionary Government which would work for a Russo-German conjunction. Hardinge rejected this advice. He did not believe that Russia would drift into Germany's arms and he realized that the Cabinet would never accept an alliance. He wrote a memorandum on 4 May 1909 in which he insisted that the British people would never agree to an alliance with Russia, especially if a reactionary Government was in power at St Petersburg. He added that he did not fear a possible return to isolation, provided that England maintained her naval supremacy, and rejected Germany's advances. Much of this was written with an eye to the Cabinet, with its 'doctrinaire ideals'[60]—indeed the memorandum was praised by Asquith and Grey—for he admitted privately that 'were we to find ourselves in a position of isolation, the situation would become very serious and we should find in Europe a combination worse than that which existed in the Napoleonic era'.[61] Later he wrote that 'my sole aim is to keep things going on the present lines so long as this Government remains in office'.[62]

The Baghdad Railway

However, Isvolsky and Prime Minister Stolypin remained in power, enabling Grey to justify continued co-operation with 'liberal' Russia. Such co-operation was never easy, especially, as has been shown, in Persia, while Turkey also provided frequent opportunities for Anglo-Russian misunderstandings and quarrels. Down to 1912 the two countries were often at cross-purposes in their policies towards the Baghdad Railway, the construction of which threatened the interests of both countries in the Middle East.

After 1907 the German-controlled railway company began to plan further extensions of the line through Mesopotamia to its ultimate destination. Grey and his advisers feared that without British participation, the railway would have a serious effect on the British trading monopoly in Mesopotamia. They were also very worried about the harm a branch from Baghdad to the Gulf would have on British strategic interests in Persia and in the Gulf. They did not believe that it would be used to convey German or Turkish troops to the Indian frontier, but they did believe that it would encourage Germany's already growing influence in the whole region. As Minto put it in March 1908:

> Given paramount German influence in Turkey, Asia Minor, Meso-
> potamia and Southern Persia our position in India would be seri-
> ously threatened and . . . we should be blind not to recognise the
> possibility of some future alliance between Russia and Germany.[63]

During Abdul Hamid's autocracy little could be done to per-suade the Turks to grant Britain concessions in the line, and attempts to reach agreement with Germany foundered on Grey's insistence that all negotiations should be conducted between Ger-many, France, Russia and Britain. Germany preferred individual negotiations to discussions *à quatre*, which would leave her in a possible minority of one. Thus an agreement which Haldane reached with the German Emperor at Windsor in November 1907 for Anglo-German negotiations on the railway collapsed when Grey insisted on his *à quatre* condition.[64] In August 1908 Hardinge hoped, in vain, that the Young Turks would cancel the Baghdad Railway Company's concession.

During 1909 the British struggled to maintain their waning influence at Constantinople, and Hardinge bombarded Lowther with instructions to do all in his power to encourage the Young Turks to look to England for advice and support, for, 'if they do not meet with sympathy and cannot learn to lean on us they will

soon learn to lean upon some other Power and the splendid position which we had at Constantinople a few months ago will be
lost'.[65] Hardinge's optimism was short-lived. After 1909 the pro-
German Nationalists began to oust the Liberals from control of
the Committee of Union and Progress, and adopted a programme
of centralization and Ottomanization for the Empire, which united
all the nationalities against them. Little progress was made with
the promised reforms. The Turks distrusted Russia, and regarded
the Triple Alliance as a far stronger combination than the Triple
Entente. As a result Germany began to recover her influence at
Constantinople. By the summer of 1910 Grey was complaining
that 'the Turks are continually doing unreasonable things and
they are on the brink of great financial difficulty. Overweening
ambition, arbitrary conduct and financial straits combined are a
dangerous mixture.'[66]

It was the Baghdad Railway more than any other question
which contributed to the deterioration of Anglo-Turkish relations in these years. Appeals to Turkish goodwill to assist Britain
to secure concessions in the line having come to nothing, Hardinge resolved to take more drastic steps. When Turkey applied
to the Powers in 1909 to allow her to increase her customs duties
by 4 per cent, Hardinge countered by demanding, in return for
Britain's agreement, a Turkish concession to England for the
construction of a railway from the Gulf to Baghdad, with an
option to extend it further into Mesopotamia. Hardinge reasoned
that Germany, faced with the prospect of a rival British line,
would agree to British control of the Gulf section of the Baghdad
Railway, which was now assuming in British eyes a greater importance than the rest of the line. Lowther did not enhance his
waning popularity in London by severely criticizing the scheme.
He thought that the Baghdad Railway would encourage the expansion of trade in the Middle East and that British traders, if
they exerted themselves, could benefit by taking advantage of their
long-standing market there. Both Germany and Turkey would,
he believed, strongly resent a British attempt to blackmail them.
Morley supported him. He told Grey that such a policy would be
regarded by Germany as most provocative—'the F.O. is too anti-
German just as not so many years ago it was too anti-French'.[67]
Both men suggested a direct approach to Germany for a settlement. Grumbling at Lowther's unhelpfulness, Hardinge never-

theless persisted in his demand throughout 1910, but without much success, since the Turks refused to consider granting the British a rival concession to the Baghdad Railway.

By 1909 Grey and Hardinge had repented of their insistence on *à quatre* negotiations, which stood in the way of an agreement with Germany. While France was quite prepared to agree to separate negotiations, Russia clung to her opposition to the railway, on the grounds that it threatened her security and trade in the Middle East. Nicolson urged Isvolsky to give way and consent to a settlement with Germany, but without success. The Russian Foreign Minister protested strenuously when he discovered that towards the end of 1909 British and German financiers had been discussing a private settlement of the question. Isvolsky accused the British of disregarding Russian interests, and of abandoning the *à quatre* stance. The Anglo-German talks came to nothing when Germany insisted on an Anglo-German political and neutrality agreement as her price for a railway agreement, an attitude to which she clung in 1910, and which made it impossible for England to contemplate a settlement with her.[68]

Russia's policy towards the Baghdad Railway changed in the autumn of 1910, when Sazonov became Foreign Minister. Anxious for a diplomatic success, he arranged a meeting of the Russian and German Emperors and their Foreign Ministers at Potsdam in November 1910. His evasions about the meeting and about what was to be discussed there filled Grey's officials with alarm. They had good reason to be concerned. At the meeting Sazonov agreed to end Russia's opposition to the completion of the Baghdad Railway while Kiderlen–Waechter for his part, agreed that Germany would not seek concessions in North Persia likely to affect Russia's strategic interests. The two men also discussed a political agreement. The details were left for subsequent negotiations between Sazonov and the German Ambassador at St Petersburg. Kiderlen wanted improved Russo-German relations, while Sazonov hoped to preserve Russia's monopoly in North Persia by preventing the construction of German controlled railways there.

The French and the British were extremely angry, and with good reason, when news of the Potsdam proceedings reached them. Not only had Sazonov failed to keep his friends informed as to what he had been discussing at Potsdam, but he had in effect

promised not to support England in any future discussions with
Germany about the line. They also feared that further concessions might yet be squeezed out of Sazonov. Cartwright asked 'is
it not time that Russia should do something spontaneously to . . .
revive the flagging energy of the Triple Entente?'[69] Nicolson ful-
minated about Sazonov's unreliability—'he appears to have been
completely hypnotized by Berlin'[70]—and Grey even threatened
to resign in favour of a pro-German Foreign Secretary. Nevertheless, both men realized that it was too late to reverse the agreement: in Cambon's words 'we must look upon what has been
done at Potsdam as a loss to be written off'.[71]

The Russians used Germany's Moroccan preoccupations in the
summer of 1911 to bring the negotiations to a rapid conclusion on
19 August, and to strike out a German-inspired political formula,
which, had it become known to Grey, would certainly have spelt
the end of the Entente. The Foreign Office recognized that Germany had secured another diplomatic success. Nevertheless, there
were grounds for optimism. Sir George Buchanan, Nicolson's
successor at St Petersburg, reported that during the latter stages
of the negotiations the Russians had genuinely tried to minimize
the harm done at Potsdam, had kept him fully informed about
developments, and he was convinced that both Sazonov and his
deputy Neratov remained at heart loyal supporters of the Entente.[72]

At least Russia was no longer an obstacle to British efforts to
secure a settlement of the Baghdad Railway, and they continued to
strive for a direct agreement with the Turks. While Nicolson
was 'not a great believer in the new [Young Turk] régime',[73]
even fearing that a strong reformed Turkey might become a
serious menace to Anglo-Russian interests in the Middle East, he
perceived that Hardinge's bullying tactics had accomplished little
beyond alienating the Turks, and driving them more and more
into the arms of the Triple Alliance. Towards the end of 1910,
therefore, the British reverted to a policy of concession and con-
ciliation in their dealings with Constantinople, in the hope that
the Turks, suspicious of Germany's intrigue at Potsdam, and in
desperate need of French loan, might reciprocate. Nicolson formulated a set of proposals about the Baghdad Railway which
included the abandonment, not only of Hardinge's attempt to
secure a rival concession, but also of the British claim for the

absolute control of the Gulf section. As an additional sop to Turkish nationalism Britain was prepared also to recognize Turkey's sovereignty over Kuweit, provided that the Sheikh remained autonomous. Once Turkey had agreed to favourable terms for British entry into the Gulf section, Britain would approve the 4 per cent customs increase. On 1 March 1911 Turkey offered to internationalize the Gulf section, alloting 40 per cent of the shares to herself and 20 per cent each to Germany, France and England.

The new Grey–Nicolson policy of conciliating the Young Turks earned them the severe criticisms of Hardinge, Bertie and Goschen, who regarded the Turkish offer as having been inspired by Germany with the ultimate object of securing control of the whole Middle East. Goschen wrote to Hardinge on 28 March that:

> Our radical wing in the Cabinet seems to want peace at any price and don't care tuppence in their short sight about our prestige in the Persian Gulf and Mesopotamia. But I have hopes that your views will put a little stiffness into the backs of those in the Cabinet who know what is right but fear to carry it out.[74]

Hardinge and Morley (who deputized for Crewe at the Indian Office during the latter's illness in 1911), attacked any settlement of the Baghdad railway which was not based on Britain's absolute control of the Gulf section, and on the maintenance of British preponderance in the Persian Gulf. The Viceroy believed that any concession over Kuweit would encourage Turkey to assert herself in the entire Gulf region, and would eventually enable her to menace India, and he called for forceful measures to resist her. 'The sooner we give Turkey a slap in the face in the Persian Gulf ... the better will be the result.'[75]

In fact Hardinge and the others were over-anxious. Grey and Nicolson were not prepared to accept what they regarded as Turkey's meagre offer of 1 March 1911, nor were they prepared to abandon Kuweit entirely to the Turks. On the other hand, Turkey had begun to embark on a programme of naval expansion, and with Britain's naval position in the Mediterranean under increasing strain, she had no wish to drive Turkey into the ranks of the Triple Alliance. Also, as it became clear from a meeting of the C.I.D. on 4 May 1911, the General Staff had no desire to become involved in hostilities with Turkey on the Gulf, should Turkey adopt a threatening attitude there. And finally, as Grey pointed out to Hardinge on 16 May 1911, the Baghdad Railway would be built with or without the customs increase, and it was therefore worthwhile making a serious effort to secure favourable terms for British entry. On 29 July 1911, therefore, Grey informed the Turks that he was prepared to accept a settlement on the basis of a 20 per cent share each for Turkey, Germany, France, Russia and England in the Gulf section, thus giving the Triple Entente a majority of the shares. If Turkey renounced interest in Bahrein, Muscat and other Gulf areas, Britain would adhere to her promise to recognize Turkish sovereignty over Kuweit. While Crewe and Hardinge persisted with their opposition to anything less than a 50 per cent British participation, Grey and Nicolson continued with their efforts in 1912, encouraged by the belief that the Italo-Turkish war might make the Turks more disposed to friendly relations.[76]

The Tripoli War

The controversy over the Baghdad railway and the Gulf took place against a steadily deteriorating background within Turkey. The Turks were still beset by domestic difficulties, and there were uprisings in the Yemen, and also in Albania, which all onlookers feared would eventually engulf the entire Balkan Peninsular. However, the first serious threat to Turkish integrity since 1908 came, not from one of her traditional enemies, but from Italy. Italy had long had her eye on Tripoli as a suitable area for colonization. On 28 September 1911, when France appeared to be well on the way to securing Morocco, Italy despatched a military expedition to Tripoli.[77]

The British had for long anticipated some Italian *coup* against the Turks, for the two countries had been squabbling for years about Italy's efforts to penetrate the province. Grey, however, had anticipated that Italy's actions would be of a punitive nature, designed to secure better treatment for her subjects and trade in Tripoli, and perhaps to secure the promise of the reversion of the province should the Turks decide to sell it. Thus he was considerably irritated when he discovered that Italy intended the forcible seizure of Tripoli from Turkey. Hardinge summed up the general feeling of disgust—'I have never heard of a worse case of brigandage than the seizure of Tripoli.'[78] Nevertheless, the British contrived to swallow their indignation. They had no wish to alienate Italy, whom they considered a brake on the aggressive policies of her Triple Alliance partners, and whose dreadnoughts they regarded as offsetting those of Austria, rather than threatening British security in the Mediterranean. Thus Grey wrote on 23 September that 'our attitude must be one of expectancy and neutrality. We must not throw Italy into the arms of Germany and Austria.'[79] Churchill agreed. 'Clearly we must prefer Italy to Turkey on all grounds—moral and unmoral.'[80]

Nevertheless, after the fuss he had made about Austria's annexation of Bosnia, Grey could hardly condone Italy's far more unscrupulous action. Nor did he wish to offend the Turks. British public opinion was outraged by Italy's action, and became increasingly anti-Italian as reports reached London of barbarities committed by Italian troops in Tripoli. Grey proclaimed a policy of strict British neutrality. Turkey's appeals for British mediation were ignored. Grey agreed to support any proposals for ending the war which were put forward by other powers; but since all the powers adopted the same attitude, being equally unwilling to offend either belligerent, little could be done.

The Russians caused irritation in London when, in October 1911, they tried to use Turkey's difficulties to persuade her to open the Straits to Russian warships. Tcharykov, the pro-Turkish Russian Ambassador at Constantinople offered, in return, a Russian guarantee of Constantinople and the Straits. Grey and Nicolson did not want complications of this sort, although they promised Russia that they would adhere to the pledge made to Isvolsky in 1908. However, Sazonov abandoned the Tcharykov proposal in December when it became quite clear that the Turks would never agree to it. The British were themselves embarrassed when the Turks approached them for an alliance on 31 October 1911: in conformity with Grey's policy of neutrality the Cabinet rejected this proposal, although Churchill, echoing popular feeling, believed that the Government should do something to persuade Italy to end the war.[81]

Indeed, by the end of the year, the British were betraying increasing irritation with Italy, not only because her decree of annexation of Tripoli in November put an end to all hope of a compromise settlement, but also because her inability to subdue the province needlessly prolonged the war. During the spring of 1912 the Triple Entente was working at cross-purposes—the French were upsetting the Italians by their angry reaction to Italy's seizure of their shipping in the Mediterranean, while the Russians, having failed to reach agreement with Turkey, began to conciliate Italy in the hope of enlisting her support against Austria in the Balkans. Russian suggestions for a Triple Entente initiative to secure a peace favourable to Italy caused alarm in London. Official British opinion was now turning in favour of the Turks, whose resistance in Tripoli appeared to confirm Grey's belief in Turkey's powers of recuperation. Russia's suggestions were brushed aside—Grey insisted that mediation must be based on five-power co-operation, and that the powers must not become divided into hostile blocs. This seemed the most sensible way of avoiding the sort of complications that had occurred in 1908 and 1909. The dispute dragged on until 15 October 1912 when, as a result of secret Italo-Turkish negotiations in the late summer, Italy at last came into possession of the province for which she had fought for so long.

The Tripoli war excited fears in London that the Balkan states might take advantage of Russia's difficulties to attack Turkey's European provinces. However, they made no move against Turkey, mainly because of doubt as to the outcome of the war. Instead they contented themselves with forming, under Russian auspices, a series of alliances in 1912, which eventually bound all of them, except Roumania, in a defensive and offensive league. After the Bosnian crisis Britain had adopted a secondary role in the Balkans. She had no wish to become involved in further difficulties in that area—as Nicolson wrote in October 1910, 'we have so much on our hands elsewhere that we have no wish to add to our responsibilities'.[82] Grey and his officials wanted a period of tranquillity in the Balkans after the 1908–9 crisis, and they were not therefore greatly enthusiastic about the Balkan confederation, which they foresaw was directed against Turkey, rather than as a defensive bloc against Austria, as Sazonov pretended. By 1912 they had also come to accept that Austria was sincere in her desire to preserve the status quo in the Balkans, and they now hoped for a revival of the pre-1908 Austro-Russian co-operation in the Balkans which had been so successful in maintaining peace, even if it had failed to secure reforms in Macedonia. They reasoned that the only chance of avoiding a war in the Balkans likely to involve the Great Powers was by a new Austro-Russian agreement. However, Austro-Russian antipathy had reached such a pitch by 1912 that the possibility of a genuine co-operation between them was impossible.

By the spring Russia's growing anti-Turkish attitude was causing increasing anxiety in London and Paris. Neither Britain nor France wanted to see the Ottoman Empire further weakened: France was as concerned as ever for her large investments there, while England did not want her Moslem subjects upset. Neither power wanted to be drawn into complications arising from Sazonov's policy in the Near East. As the prospect of a Balkan conflagration became more likely in the summer, Grey continued to pursue the chimera of Austro-Russian co-operation to localize the conflict. Suggestions put forward by various powers to maintain peace in the summer and autumn were wrecked on the rocks of Austro-Russian jealousy. By September, as frontier clashes between Bulgarian and Montenegrin troops and Turkey became more frequent, and as the bands provoked serious incidents in Macedonia, even Sazonov became alarmed at the likely consequences of his policy. The Balkan states were deluged with appeals from the Great Powers to maintain the peace; Turkey with appeals to introduce reforms into Macedonia immediately. Grey's final efforts to promote Austro-Russian co-operation came too late—on 1 October 1912 he wrote: 'Russia and Austria are the only Powers who can sit on the heads of the Balkan States and I see nothing more that we can do.'[83] Europe was now faced with the spectre of a serious upheaval in the Balkans, and one which might lead to a general conflagration involving the Great Powers.

Chapter 4

Anglo-American Relations, 1895–1914

> In such a war we could not possibly win—no combination of Powers could successfully invade and conquer the United States . . .
>
> A. H. Lee (of Fareham), 1905

The Myth of Anglo-American Friendship

To the German observer it often seemed that the fixation of the British upon the North Sea and the growing German High Seas Fleet, was irrational, a reflection of prejudice rather than a wise precaution. For did not the U.S.A. possess a growing fleet? Was America from 1898 onwards not more expansionist even than Germany, more of a long-term threat to British commercial predominance? Did not the relative power of Washington and Ottawa pose a threat to the British Empire: why was it only the German army and the German fleet which dominated British strategic thinking?

The answer to this question is twofold. Firstly, feelings towards America in Britain *were* irrational. Although the ideas of 'hands across the sea', 'blood is thicker than water' and the 'Pax anglo-americana', have been overdone as an explanation of the relative cordiality of relations between London and Washington, there was something in it. It was much stronger at the British end than at the American—and always remained so—but in London it meant more than after dinner speeches. Many politicians of importance—Joseph Chamberlain, Balfour, Arthur Lee, Sir Edward Grey—wanted as close a relationship with America as it was possible to obtain. They spoke the same language and thought that they shared the same inheritance. As Selborne wrote in 1905 when the defence of Canada was under discussion, he put his 'faith in the innate justice of the American people' to restrain them from attacking their northern neighbour.[1] No member of the Cabinet would have made a similar pronouncement in favour of Germany. At a lower level, Fisher, the First Sea Lord, ardently espoused this course, as did Bryce, Spring-Rice and some of the younger diplomats—like Esmé Howard and Eustace Percy. Even Hardinge, for all his cynicism, accepted that close friendship with America was essential. Garvin, editor of the *Observer*, the Milnerites, Northcliffe and Rothermere (before 1914), all shared this idealist view that the solution to Britain's problems in the twentieth century was to admit America as an equal partner in the *pax britannica*.[2] Even though this feeling was not reciprocated to anything like the same extent on the other side of the Atlantic, it obviously played a part in the formulation of British policy.

The second point was strategic planning, closely coupled with the eternal search for economy. Since the 1860s successive British Governments had abandoned the struggle for control of the North American continent, and had contented themselves with the maintenance of their existing colonies in Canada and the West Indies. From 1890 onwards, with the development of an American fleet, the Admiralty periodically observed that these colonies were no longer defensible, at least by sea, as the major strength of the British navy was always required in European waters—first against France and Russia, later against Germany.[3] Fisher, when he arrived at the Admiralty, put this view forward with all his usual energy. Not only was a war 'with our cousins across the Atlantic' most improbable, it was impossible to fight the U.S.A. close to its bases. Britain could not possibly escape 'an overwhelming and humiliating defeat by the United States and therefore he would leave Canada to her fate'. Despite opposition from the General Staff, who had only two years before drawn up a new plan for the defence of Canada, Fisher's view prevailed in the Committee of Imperial Defence, aided by Arnold-Foster's desire to withdraw all British troops from Halifax and the West Indies in order to economize. By the spring of 1907 this was accomplished.[4] Thereafter the undefended frontier was a reality, at least as far as London was concerned.

The major answer then to the divergence in British policies towards two *apparently* similar threats, lay in the fact that in North America it was physically impossible to defend British interests. As in the case of the Russian threat to Persia, the result was therefore to seek an accommodation and call it friendship. There was also, of course, one striking difference. The German threat was to the British Isles themselves, the homeland: that from Russia or America would first be felt by imperial possessions overseas. Given this choice, concentration in Europe was inevitable.

The last British statesman to feel sufficiently confident in British power to stand up to the U.S.A. was Salisbury; and the panic that this induced amongst his colleagues was no doubt responsible for Lansdowne's readiness to concede almost anything that Washington demanded. The squabble with Venezuela over the precise boundaries of British Guiana was a dispute which had no great urgency: it had been in progress since the founding of Venezuela. But it acquired importance when, in July 1895, the U.S. Secretary of State, Olney, sent a note to London asserting the right of the U.S.A. under the Monroe Doctrine to intervene to settle any dispute between a European power and an American state. Olney insisted that England should submit the boundary question to arbitration. Salisbury, who had more pressing problems in July 1895 and regarded Venezuela as of no importance, took four months to reply. When he did, he denied that the Monroe Doctrine had any bearing on this dispute and politely reminded Olney that in any case the *obiter dicta* of President Monroe had no standing in international law as they had never been accepted by the powers. Britain, he added, had always been willing to submit the question to arbitration, except for the part of the territory which had been in continual British occupation since the closing years of the Spanish Empire.[5]

There Salisbury would have left it; but President Cleveland, annoyed by the long delay and aware of the popularity which a public stand would bring him, announced in a message to Congress on 17 December 1895 that he upheld the U.S. right to intervene and was appointing a commission to report on the question. If the report were unfavourable to Britain, he told Congress, he would insist that she evacuate any Venezuelan territory she had occupied illegally. This declaration naturally enough, was music to the ears of the Irish and other anti-British elements in America: fortunately the Kruger telegram distracted British jingoes in another direction. Nevertheless, the prospect of a war with the United States over an issue of this character, at a time when Canadian defences were in a poor state and England was completely isolated in Europe, so alarmed the Cabinet that on 11 January

1896 Joseph Chamberlain led a revolt: there were to be negotiations with Washington to find a definitive settlement. The ensuing discussions dragged on for months until the original issue had been almost forgotten—Venezuela was barely consulted—but at last on 12 November 1896 an Anglo-Venezuelan treaty was signed. By the terms of this, Venezuela was to accept the award of an Anglo-American boundary commission on her frontier with Guiana, whilst most of the area claimed by the British was excluded from consideration. By the award on 30 October 1899, British Guiana in fact secured the bulk of the area she had always claimed. Of course, as a result of this action Britain accepted the validity of the Monroe Doctrine which Salisbury had tried to deny:

> the recognition of the quasi U.S. Protectorate over the whole of America (which is the obvious result of admitting their claim to interfere in our quarrel with Venezuela) is a step which must have far-reaching consequences.[6]

Historians have paid considerable attention to the steady improvement in Anglo-American relations which followed the settlement of the Venezuelan crisis.[7] Certainly there was a relaxation of the state of suspicion—acute at times—which had been evident since the war of independence. Nevertheless, the *rapprochement* was much more apparent than real—a product of myth making and wishful thinking. Those sections of public opinion in the two countries which believed in ties of affinity and sentiment as a basis of foreign relations aligned the two countries in a common accord. To some extent this was true; but what really happened was that—as with the Japanese alliance and the French Entente—public opinion obligingly followed the dictates of sheer necessity for Britain. Since there could be no question of resisting American pretensions to the hegemony of the 'New World'— especially at a time when Britain was fully occupied in South Africa and seriously worried by Russian advances in Manchuria— Britain swallowed her indignation and accepted American friendship on the best terms available.

Thus during the Spanish-American war of 1898, the myth arose in the United States that England had prevented a German-led Europe from intervening on the side of Spain. The reality was otherwise. The European powers were too divided to present a

united front and no power was willing to risk American dis-
pleasure for the sake of a derelict country like Spain. The British
ships at Manila were there to protect British interests in the
Philippines and observe U.S. tactics, not to protect Admiral
Dewey from a German attack. Balfour decided to remain aloof
from the schemes to propose mediation to the United
States, but this no more meant that Britain was pro-American
than similar action in the Sino-Japanese war indicated any support for Japan. In fact Pauncefote, the British Ambassador in
Washington, tried to mobilize a collective note among the diplomatic corps in favour of accepting Spanish offers of a Cuban
settlement, but Balfour vetoed his action just in time. If the
American public had learnt of this initiative, presumably less
would have been heard of British friendship. The American
annexations of the Philippines and Cuba were not greeted with
any pleasure in official circles in London, as both the Admiralty
and War Office thought these actions a danger to British interests. The only consolation to be found was that annexation by
Germany would have been infinitely worse.

Nor was there any prospect, as Joseph Chamberlain hoped, of
an alliance between the two countries. This would have been an
impossible departure from American traditions and, besides, all
the advantages would have lain with Britain. The Royal Navy was
bound to protect the United States in the unlikely event of an
attack from a major European power; British interests alone
would demand this. Even in an area where American and British
interests were reasonably identical—China—Washington would
never consider the use of force to uphold their common interests
until obliged to by sheer necessity in 1941. An approach to this
end in 1898 was turned down. Equally, the American solution of
moral exhortation—Hay's 'open door' notes of 1899 and 1900—
was an embarrassment in London since it conflicted with the
British intention of protecting her interests in China by concessions, 'spheres of influence' agreements, and an alliance with Japan.

In North and Central America acute problems remained to
divide the two countries after 1900. The most pressing was the
project for an isthmian canal which, after years of discussion, was
at last becoming a practical possibility. By the Clayton-Bulwer
treaty of 1850 England and the United States had agreed that any
future canal linking the Pacific and Atlantic oceans should be

internationally built and operated. By 1900, however, Washington, conscious of its new-found strength and aware from its recent experiences of war against Spain what an advantage sole control of such a canal would bring, wanted to re-write the treaty.

In London the Admiralty were totally opposed to a canal under sole U.S. control, as it would give the Americans the immense advantage, in an Anglo-American war, of the ability to switch their fleets from one ocean to another. Lansdowne, however, realizing that England was in no position to prevent construction anyway, decided to give way and re-negotiate the 1850 treaty. Salisbury, when faced with this request in 1898, had made it a pre-condition that Washington should first make a reasonable settlement of the long-standing dispute over the Alaskan boundary, but Lansdowne dropped this demand. By 1900 Britain was in too isolated a position to risk a major dispute with the U.S.A., especially as it appeared in a War Office study that British Columbia—the province directly affected by the dispute—was indefensible against an American attack. Consequently, by the Hay-Pauncefote treaty of 18 November 1901 the U.S.A. was given the right to build, operate and defend the canal, without England getting anything in exchange apart from a clause forbidding discriminatory tolls on foreign shipping.

The natural result was that when the Alaskan boundary came up for settlement during the Presidency of Theodore Roosevelt, London had no possible lever to exert upon Washington. In 1903 an American proposal that they set up a tribunal of six to adjudicate on the Alaska boundary was accepted in London and Ottawa. Of the three Americans, Roosevelt appointed two politicians—one, Senator Lodge, was hardly noted for his fair-mindedness to foreigners, and the other was the Secretary for War. Only one U.S. representative was a jurist. Canada, with misplaced generosity, appointed two jurists, while London sent Lord Alverstone, Lord Chief Justice of England. The result was a foregone conclusion: on a majority vote the United States was assigned practically the whole area under dispute. Alverstone—it was said on instructions from London—voted with the majority. Though this result led to great indignation in Canada, in fact England had settled her last major dispute in North America and was thankful for it. Selborne was speaking for the Cabinet, if not for the nation, when he announced in 1905 that there is no party in the United Kingdom nor even in the British Empire which does not contemplate a war with the United States of America as the greatest evil which could befall the British Empire in its foreign relations.[8]

Grey and the Liberals were, if anything, even more committed to good relations with Washington than their predecessors, especially as it enabled them to make further reductions in military and naval expenditure. There were minor problems—the difficulty of reconciling the alliance with Japan and friendship with America, especially Japanese-Russian irritation at Taft's dollar diplomacy in North China;[9] and a momentary squall when the Senate in 1912 exempted U.S. shipping from Panama canal tolls, a direct violation of the 1901 treaty. (This disappeared when Woodrow Wilson persuaded Congress to drop the clause in 1914.) But these were relatively minor matters compared with the one problem which did bring serious difficulties, Mexico.

The Mexican Revolution

The Mexican revolution of 1911 led to three years of Anglo-American controversy.[10] Under the dictatorship of Porfirio Diaz, Mexico had enjoyed a period of relative internal stability since 1870. Diaz had encouraged foreign investment in an effort to build up a modern economy. The bulk of this came from the United States as Britain, who had up to mid-century enjoyed commercial supremacy in Mexico, lost out after 1876. The only exception lay in the oil industry. Here Britain seriously challenged American supremacy. Encouraged by Diaz, who was eager to counter the U.S. near-monopoly of investment, a British engineer named Pearson, later Lord Cowdray, entered the Mexican oil industry in 1901. To the annoyance of his American competitors, in 1906 he was granted a drilling lease over a large area of Mexico, a lease which paid considerable dividends and gave him a large stake in the political stability of the country.

By 1906 there was mounting opposition to Diaz from the peasantry, who had not drawn any benefit from the growth of Mexican industries and who were afflicted by the age-old problem of the concentration of land ownership in a few hands. Equally, the educated middle class were alienated by his encouragement of American control of most of Mexican industry. This dual opposition came to a head under the leadership of Francisco Madero, a liberal landowner, who believed that only by restoring democracy —in place of dictatorship—could the condition of the people be improved. By 1911 the opposition had produced sporadic revolutionary episodes all over Mexico, outbreaks which so alarmed President Taft that, for the sake of American investments, he mobilized 20,000 troops along the border. Clearly the object of this action was to intervene on the side of Diaz.

In the event Taft changed his mind and in May 1911 Diaz, with the help of Cowdray, fled the country. In October Madero was voted President. His victory was accompanied by a campaign in the press by the American oil interests calling on the new Government to cancel Cowdray's leases on the grounds of his identification with the former régime. Madero, however, promised to respect the Diaz concessions and, if he had been able to control his own followers, might have had a chance of establishing a Government of reform and progress. But many would not wait for his gradualist approach to bring benefits and in 1912 the revolution was renewed against the revolutionary President. Madero, forced to rely on the military commander, General Huerta, to restore order, found that he had gone for a ride on a tiger, for in February 1913 Huerta had the President arrested and, probably, murdered. Huerta now became provisional President. This was done on the direct encouragement of the U.S. ambassador, Henry Lane Wilson, who claimed that Madero was anti-American: presumably because he would not cancel Cowdray's concession.

Until 1913 Grey had paid little attention to Latin America. Apart from his distractions elsewhere, U.S. preponderance there was an accepted fact and no attempt had been made to obstruct Roosevelt or Taft in their expansionist mood.[11] But in March 1913 he rushed to give limited diplomatic recognition to the new provisional President of Mexico, with the simple object of protecting Cowdray's concession. This had become all important to the Government in London and in July Cowdray's company— Anglo-Mexican Oil Products—was given long-term Admiralty contracts. The Admiralty needed the oil and it appeared that only Huerta could provide the necessary political stability for them to obtain it.

The difficulties began when Woodrow Wilson succeeded Taft

to the Presidency of the U.S.A. The new President, rejecting the policies of his predecessors, determined that the U.S.A. must identify with democratic régimes in the American continent. As a recent writer has put it:

> He was sure that America must take a part, indeed the most important part, on the international scene. The United States had an obligation to present an example of good government at home and fair dealing abroad.[12]

Wilson soon perceived that the Huerta régime conflicted with this ideal for democracy throughout the Americas, as the General had seized power and murdered the legitimate President, all with the connivance, if not the inspiration, of the American Ambassador. Recalling his Ambassador in August 1913, President Wilson announced his refusal to recognize the Huerta government unless the General retired from office and held new elections in a truly democratic climate. To give effect to this programme Wilson sent a special emissary, John Lind, to negotiate with the various parties in Mexico.

This opposition to the Huerta government encouraged what remained of the Madero faction and, as Grey feared, led to revolts in northern Mexico in 1913 which threatened to plunge the whole country into renewed civil war. To add to Grey's difficulties, Woodrow Wilson was convinced that Cowdray—who had friends in the British Government—and Grey were collaborating to uphold Huerta and to promote British oil interests at the expense of those of the United States. In fact this assumption was unfounded, yet Grey would not withdraw his limited recognition of Huerta nor would he agree to joint pressure upon the General to enforce Wilson's demands. The most he would do was to observe a strict neutrality, promising Wilson to hold over *complete* recognition until elections had been held in November. Privately, he advised Huerta to receive Lind; but the General, somewhat irate at Wilson's high handedness, refused to do so until he had been recognized by Washington.

Grey's difficulties were increased by the fact that the new British Minister to Mexico, Sir Lionel Carden, was an outspoken critic of American commercial policy in Central and South America, and advocated strenuous British efforts to regain her lost pre-eminence in this field. He urged upon the Foreign Office that they support the now anti-American Huerta and frustrate Wilson's efforts to unseat him and to establish a thinly disguised pro-U.S. régime. To Grey such action seemed impossible as, if it came to the point, England could not give Huerta effective aid against the U.S.A. and consequently he ordered Carden not to adopt any line independent of that of his U.S. colleague.

In October 1913 the General closed the Mexican Congress. This action, Lind believed, had been encouraged by Carden and Cowdray, a belief which was supported by Carden's action on 22 October when he gave a press interview which was highly critical of American policy, attacking Wilson's demand for immediate elections in Mexico as unrealistic. This statement caused an uproar in the U.S.A. and led Secretary of State William Jennings Bryan to protest to London that Britain was encouraging Huerta's undemocratic proceedings. This Grey denied. He pointed out that Huerta had promised to hold new elections, and insisted that England would decide on whether or not to extend full recognition only when these had been held, as he had previously promised Washington. In fact the elections were held on 26 November and resulted in a massive vote for the General, showing that Huerta had certainly mastered the art, if not the spirit, of democracy.

During November 1913 the tension between England and the United States over Mexico began to relax. Grey had no intention of envenoming relations over this question; for him it was simply a conflict between traditional British diplomatic methods and Wilson's peculiar moral principles. Grey believed that Wilson had not given sufficient consideration to his policy before embarking upon a condemnation of Huerta since, if the General fell, Mexico would relapse into anarchy and Wilson would find himself forced to intervene. This, he presumed, Wilson wished to avoid. The outcome in fact was a resounding diplomatic defeat for Washington since Huerta, far from resigning, went from strength to strength and Lind had to leave Mexico with nothing accomplished.

Though at first inclined to blame Britain for this fiasco, Bryan and Wilson gradually came to accept Grey's assurances that he and Cowdray were not in league to control Mexican oil and defy the United States. Bryan even came to believe that Grey had altered his policy from one of opposition to one of support for

America. While no doubt this belief was useful to Britain's moral reputation in Washington on the eve of the war, it was completely unfounded. In fact Grey had maintained a fairly consistent policy in Mexico since 1912—one of limited recognition of Huerta in order to protect British commercial interests. He had at no stage embarked upon a policy of opposition to the U.S.: this was Carden's doing, in excess of his instructions, and, significantly, he was recalled in August 1914.

The wisdom of this policy was soon apparent. From 1914–18 there was a steady flow of oil for Cowdray's Admiralty contracts, despite the increasing American embroilment in Mexican affairs. Equally, Grey's reputation stood high in Washington on the eve of the European war, which it would certainly not have done if he had followed Carden's prompting and embarked on a contest for commercial supremacy in Central and South America. Wilson's speech at Mobile on 28 October 1913 was clear enough in intention: henceforward the Monroe Doctrine was to have economic clauses, 'foreign' powers should not be granted concessions in America's backyard.

Chapter 5

Britain and Europe, 1912–14

I begin to hope that it has once more been possible
owing to Anglo-German collaboration to save the peace
of Europe.

Prince Lichnowsky, 28 July 1914

The Balkan Wars[1]

As the tension between Turkey and the Balkan states increased
during the autumn of 1912, the Powers redoubled their belated
efforts to secure a peaceful settlement of the Macedonian question. On 8 October Austria and Russia temporarily overcame
their mutual antagonism and presented, on behalf of the Concert
of Europe, a note warning the Balkan States that they would not
allow any changes to take place in the territorial status quo in the
Balkans. On the same day Montenegro declared war on Turkey.[2]
Nicolson complained that 'the primary cause of all this trouble
was Sazonov instigating the Balkan States to make alliances and
parcel out Macedonia'.[3] During the following week Serbia, Bulgaria and Greece opened hostilities with Turkey.

By early November the Turkish armies had suffered a series of
shattering defeats at the hands of the allies, and had been driven
out of Macedonia. The bulk of her forces fell back on Constantinople, although a few garrisons held out in Adrianople,
Janina, Scutari and Durazzo. The allied victories were greeted
with considerable enthusiasm in England, and some Cabinet
Ministers were delighted that the cause of the Balkan nationalities
had at last triumphed.[4] The Foreign Office was determined that
no official partiality should be displayed towards the Balkan
states, since this might antagonize the Moslem subjects of the
British Empire. Nor did the British want to drive the Turks into
total dependence on Germany. On the other hand there could
now be no question of the Powers attempting to deprive the Balkan allies of the territory they had conquered, and this decision

was confirmed by Asquith in a speech at the Guildhall on 9 November 1912.

The major British anxiety was that Austria might intervene to obtain some advantage for herself in the Balkans, or to deprive Serbia of some of her gains. Austria watched the momentous changes that were taking place on her borders with increasing alarm. While the Austrian Crown Council ruled out Austrian military involvement, Berchtold, the new Austrian Foreign Minister, felt that his country must make some reservations about the future shape of the Balkans in order to safeguard her interests there, and to assert her right to exercise a major part in any subsequent settlement. He could only fall back on a plan that had been drawn up by the Ballplatz in the late 1890s, which provided for the establishment of an autonomous Albania on the shores of the Adriatic, in the event of the collapse of Turkey-in-Europe. This plan would not only restrict Serbia's territorial gains, but would also exclude her from the Adriatic coast. He pretended that a Serbian Adriatic port might be used as a naval base by the barely-existent Russian fleet, but in reality he hoped that her exclusion from the Adriatic would reduce Serbia's economic independence and lower her prestige.[5] Italy, who was equally determined that Serbia should not gain a foothold on the Adriatic coast, and who suspected Austria of having her own ambitions there, supported Berchtold's Albanian proposals.

Russia was equally unwilling to be dragged into war over the Balkans, yet Russian Pan-Slav feeling and Russia's prestige compelled Sazonov to make a show of support for Serbia's clamour to be left in occupation of all the territory she had captured from the Turks. Thus throughout the next few months Europe was faced with a series of Austro-Russian squabbles over Albania, which threatened to lead to a confrontation similar to that of 1909, but with no certainty that on this occasion Russia would again yield.

Grey had no wish to support Russia even to the same limited extent as he had in 1909, especially as Serbia was now in possession of large areas of Macedonia, the bulk of which she would probably retain. Nor was Germany willing to become too closely involved on Austria's side. Hence Grey was delighted when Kiderlen suggested that the two countries should co-operate to prevent the Balkan Wars from escalating into a conflict between the Great Powers.[6] The Foreign Office regarded Grey's enthusiastic reception of the German approach with some concern, especially since Sazonov made it clear that he expected British diplomatic support in the Balkans. Nicolson, Crowe and the others delivered their usual warnings to Grey about Germany's efforts to weaken the Ententes:

> We should take very great care . . . to keep closely in touch with Russia and endeavour to harmonise our action as far as possible with hers. If we do not do this I much fear that the outcome will be a very serious weakening. if indeed not the break-up of the Triple Entente, and this would leave Germany the absolute arbiter of the whole situation.[7]

Although Grey persisted with his efforts to reach a peaceful settlement of the Balkan crisis, he was not unmindful of Nicolson's warnings: while he was prepared to try to reconcile the conflicting views of Austria and Russia, he realized he could not go too far in opposition to Russia. He wrote to Bertie on 30 October:

> The prospect of a Turkish 'debâcle' and the complete victory of the Balkan States makes things more difficult. Public opinion here will be dead against turning the Balkan States out of what they may show their ability to conquer by their own forces. If Russia and Austria do agree upon a settlement, public opinion here will not push its own views and force the Government to assert them. But if Austria were to attack the Balkan States and Russia said 'Hands Off', it would be impossible for a British Government, even if it desired, to side diplomatically with Austria against Russia. I propose to work for agreement between Russia and Austria, but it will have to be with the limitation that Austria is reasonable.[8]

While Austria and Italy were pressing for the establishment of an independent Albania, another issue arose during November which was fraught with even more serious consequences for European peace. By early November the Bulgarians seemed to be on the point of capturing Constantinople. Whatever sympathy Sazonov entertained for the aspirations of the Balkan states elsewhere in the Peninsular, he was totally opposed to the domination of Constantinople and the Straits by Bulgaria or indeed by any other foreign Power. Russia's industrialization programme depended on the unimpeded passage of her trade through the Straits. He therefore threatened Russian intervention to prevent a Bulgarian conquest of the Turkish capital.[9] Grey feared that the fall of Constantinople might precipitate the collapse of Turkey-in-Asia, resulting in a scramble for the spoils by the Powers. Nicolson commented later:

> There is really more risk of a European War arising out of the clash and collision of rival interests in Asia than there is in the case of the Albanian or other European question. If Europe begins to scramble over the debris of the Ottoman Empire in Asia I should be very much surprised if the scramble did not develop into an open conflict.[10]

Thus in the early months of the crisis considerable anxiety prevailed in London both about the future of Constantinople, and also in case Austria should launch a preventive attack on Serbia before the latter could consolidate her recent gains. There were a number of Austro-Serbian incidents in November which raised temperatures in both countries, and provoked both Austrian and Russian military preparations. On 8 November Lord Stamfordham reported to the King that Asquith 'thinks the situation may become very serious and that he looks upon it as being worse than has yet been the case',[11] while Lloyd George, Seely and Churchill were equally worried.[12] Soon Asquith, Lloyd George and Churchill were urging Grey that 'we ought to take some initiative of our own' to safeguard England's 'future position in the Near East',[13] but precisely what Grey could do under the circumstances was far from clear. The Cabinet, on 6 November, somewhat weakly suggested British mediation to end the fighting around Constantinople,[14] and failing this Asquith and Grey suggested that if the capital fell, England should demand that it be internationalized, a proposal which, as the French pointed out, was hardly likely to appeal to the Russians. Grey's pressure on the Bulgarians not to force the Turkish defences (the Tchaldja Lines) was ignored, but the crisis subsided when the Bulgarians failed to capture the city.

Albania remained the chief difficulty. While Russia was eventually induced to accept the establishment of an autonomous Albania, she continued to support Serbian and Montenegrin claims to as much as possible of the area. Austria on the other hand, for the opposite reason, was determined to establish a large Albania. Thus Europe was faced with a series of acute crises over the future of a few villages in Albania, whose names and exact geographical locations were known only to a few experts.

Grey decided to support Austria's refusal to allow Serbia an Adriatic port for, as he pointed out to Benckendorff on 26 November, the issue was not worth a European war. Three days later he informed Prince Lichnowsky, the new German Ambassador, that 'Germany, France and England must all have the same feeling: that it would be intolerable if they were drawn into a war about something that did not matter to any of them'.[15] His officials agreed. Nicolson thought that 'it would be supremely ridiculous if Europe were to be involved in a war over such a petty question',[16] while Goschen considered it 'perfectly outrageous that we should all be kept on tenterhooks because of Serbia's ambitions . . . She is going to have a large slice of cake and now wants to go to war because there's not enough sugar on it!'[17]

Nicolson continued to fear that Grey's favourable response to Germany's approach for joint co-operation in the Balkans might lead Germany to gamble on British neutrality in the event of war. He wrote to Hardinge on 21 November that 'I sincerely trust that the Cabinet will not be led away in this direction, though it requires a great deal of watchfulness to prevent them from doing so.'[18] Grey was not unaware of the danger. He made it clear to Lichnowsky that his efforts to promote a peaceful settlement of the dispute would be frustrated if Germany decided on all-out support for Austria. A speech by Bethmann Hollweg on 2 December had been widely interpreted in this sense.[19] The King told Prince Henry of Prussia, who visited Sandringham in December, that under certain circumstances, England would come to the aid of France and Russia in the event of a continental war. Grey wrote to the King that

> If Austria attacked Servia aggressively and Germany attacked Russia if she came to the assistance of Servia and France was then involved, it might become necessary for England to fight.

Haldane gave a similar warning to Lichnowsky on 6 December.[20]
Nevertheless, Grey was not without hope that a settlement would be reached. The prospects appeared to be a little brighter when, on 3 December, the allies and Turkey agreed to an armistice and to hold a peace conference in London, which opened at St James's Palace on 16 December. On the following day a conference of Ambassadors, with Grey in the chair, was convened at

the Foreign Office. Grey had already persuaded the other Great Powers that while the allies and Turkey should negotiate a Balkan settlement amongst themselves, the Great Powers should reserve the right to make a final decision on a number of sensitive questions, including the extent and organization of Albania, and the future of the Aegean Islands. The Ambassadorial conference, originally an Anglo-German suggestion, was intended as an informal body to make recommendations on these questions to the several Governments.[21] Grey wrote later:

> My own part in this Conference seems very drab and humdrum in recollection. British interests were not affected by the destiny of Djakova or Scutari, and my part was not to initiate or shape a policy, but to serve as a useful and patient mediator between Russia and Austria, to be diligent in finding the point of conciliation and burying the point of difference.[22]

The work of the Ambassadors was facilitated, at the outset, by Serbia's decision to abandon her demand for an Adriatic port.[23] Her retreat had been insisted upon by Sazonov, in the face of Anglo-French pressure. Grey was greatly relieved at the outcome. He wrote to Lloyd George that 'diplomatically we are past the biggest rocks and with goodwill we ought to be past the others'.[24]

His optimism was premature. The Great Powers were now presented with the problem of Scutari, which was still held by the Turks. Montenegro, whose forces were besieging the town, demanded that it should be assigned to her when the Turkish garrison surrendered. Mensdorff objected strenuously. He pointed out that Montenegro might one day be united with Serbia, and that, in any case, Scutari was clearly an Albanian town. Indeed he insisted that all towns inhabited by Albanians ought to be assigned to Albania. Benckendorff supported the claims of Montenegro, and Sazonov informed Grey that, after his concession regarding Serbia's port, he could hardly give way over Scutari as well. Grey told Lichnowsky on 18 December that he hoped that, under the circumstances Germany would persuade Austria to abandon Scutari to Montenegro, but this Austria refused to do.

By the end of the year the peace conference of the allies and Turkey was deadlocked over another issue—Bulgaria's demand that Turkey should cede Adrianople, which Bulgaria had been unable to capture during the war. In an effort to prevent the renewal of hostilities various measures were suggested to persuade Turkey to give way, ranging from an attempt to bribe Turkey by offering her two Greek occupied Aegean Isles (which the Cabinet rejected as likely to alienate Greece and create more Cretes in the Aegean),[25] to a collective naval demonstration, which Germany rejected as likely to offend Turkey. Eventually, on 17 January 1913, the Ambassadors decided to present a collective note to Turkey, urging her to cede Adrianople to Bulgaria. Lowther warned Grey that the note was unlikely to have any effect, since he believed that the German Ambassador at Constantinople was trying to curry favour with the Turks by advising them privately to ignore it. 'In London and Berlin Germany seems to be professing "to play the game" but here the professions are too thin to take in many.'[26] In fact the Turkish Cabinet was anxious to avert further hostilities by accepting the advice of the Great Powers. However, its willingness to compromise offended the extremists and on 23 January it was overthrown in a *coup d'état* by what Lowther later described as 'a handful of desperados', led by Enver Pasha, who was pro-German and anti-British in outlook.[27]

'Altogether,' as Asquith put it on 17 January, 'the prospect is somewhat more clouded.'[28] The deadlock over Scutari could not be resolved. Germany and Italy were supporting Austria's case; France that of Russia. However, after exerting much pressure throughout January Grey finally managed to persuade Sazonov, on 11 February, to allow Scutari to go to Albania, in return for Grey's promise to support him in trying to secure generous frontiers for Serbia in eastern Albania. The Russian Foreign Minister complained of the feeble British support he had received so far, and of the encouragement Grey's friendly attitude towards Germany was giving to Austrian intransigence. In his reply Grey was equally forthright:

> I should endeavour, if war broke out between Russia and Austria, to secure that Germany, France and Great Britain should all stand aside: if this failed I cannot say what would happen. It seems unreasonable and intolerable that the greater part of Europe should be involved in war for a dispute about one or two towns on the Albanian frontier.[29]

There were further Austro-Russian quarrels about the future of villages on the eastern frontier of Albania, although here Mensdorff was prepared to make concessions. Relations between the two Powers became extremely tense over one village, Djakova, during March. When, on the 5th, Berchtold agreed that its future should be decided by an international frontier commission (a body which had been suggested earlier by Grey as a means of settling such issues on an ethnographical basis), Sazonov insisted that the commission should be advised in advance to agree to its transfer to Serbia. Grey betrayed an increasing irritation with Sazonov's obstructive tactics. He was not prepared to agree that the commission should merely register Russia's demands, and more than once in despair he threatened to terminate the Ambassadorial conferences if the participants did not adopt a more flexible attitude. He warned the Russians on 17 March, 'I do not suppose that under any circumstances a war about the Albanian frontier would be regarded as a British interest involving action upon our part.'[30] On 21 March, however, Berchtold agreed to allow the transfer of Djakova to Serbia, if, in return, the Powers would co-operate to persuade Montenegro to lift the siege of Scutari, which still continued, despite frequent demands from the Powers that Montenegro abandon her efforts to subdue the town.

In order to prevent separate Austrian action to force Montenegro to raise her siege, Grey now adopted an idea earlier mentioned by Sazonov—the despatch of an international fleet to the coast as a means of bringing the Montenegrins to heel. Although the Cabinet agreed to Grey's scheme, Churchill warned the Ministers that England should 'not be drawn into any position distinct from that of France and Russia, and still less into giving any kind of support . . . in attacking Montenegro.' The Montenegrin cause was popular in England, and the Government should not appear to be giving encouragement to efforts to deprive her of the fruits of her victories.[31]

Thus Grey could not sanction the landing of British marines in Albania should the blockade fail. Nor could he diverge too far from his associates in the Triple Entente. Grey was soon faced with this prospect when, after Sazonov had agreed to the despatch of an international fleet, he refused to allow Russian ships to participate, fearing an outcry from Russian public opinion if Russia actively helped to coerce a Slav nation. Thereupon France, unwilling to risk offending her ally, also refused to send ships. Grey became increasingly angry with the failure of France and Russia to support his efforts to secure a peaceful outcome of the dispute. He complained that they 'are playing a very ignoble part that may end in the European War that they wish to avoid',[32] while the Cabinet described France's attitude as 'difficult to understand and still more difficult to defend'.[33]

Grey could not allow British warships to act alone with those of the Triple Alliance, and he warned France and Russia that, under these circumstances, he could not oppose separate Austro-Italian intervention to enforce the decision of the Great Powers. This threat sufficed to bring the two countries into line, and by 6 April an international fleet of Austrian, Italian, German, French and British warships were imposing a pacific blockade off Antivari.

Elsewhere in the Balkans further complications threatened when on 3 February the allies, having failed to secure Turkish agreement to the complete evacuation of Adrianople, resumed hostilities. Sazonov once again became alarmed as the Bulgarians renewed their assault upon Constantinople, and he demanded Triple Entente pressure to persuade Bulgaria to abandon her campaign. Grey refused on the grounds that separate action would split the Concert. In view of Russia's anxiety, however, he agreed to unilateral action by Russia to expel the Bulgarians should they enter the Turkish capital.

Meanwhile the presence of the international fleet failed to have any effect on Montenegro's efforts to reduce Scutari; indeed its futility was further demonstrated when on 23 April the town fell to the Montenegrin army. The Triple Alliance powers now demanded the landing of marines from the international fleet to dislodge the Montenegrins: Grey, faced with a possible outcry in the Liberal Party to this course, would not agree. He could only suggest as an alternative the tightening of the blockade and the offer of an international loan to Montenegro to secure her compliance. Since both these measures seemed likely to be ineffective, he next proposed limited Austrian action to expel the Montenegrins from the town:

> The course I should like to see adopted if possible would be to indicate certain limits as desirable for Austrian action, and to say that as long as [her] action was kept within those limits the reunion of Ambassadors and the naval demonstration would not be abruptly brought to an end. In this way some moderating influence would be retained over action by Austria.[34]

The difficulty was that, even if Russia agreed, Austria might be forced to go beyond limited action in order to secure a Montenegrin surrender; the result might be an Austrian invasion of Montenegro and uproar in Russia, which would lead to her intervention. Grey warned Mensdorff on 1 May that a general conflagration might ensue in which the question of Scutari would be lost sight of. 'In such an event, we and other Powers should have to consider, not the merits of the question of Scutari, but what our own interests required us to do in a European crisis.'[35] Fortunately, just as Austria was on the point of delivering an ultimatum to Montenegro, the King agreed to abandon the town, which was taken over by an international force early in May.

The situation in the Balkans remained tense throughout the spring. Turkey, again defeated in the second round of hostilities with the allies, sued for peace, and on 30 May 1913, after considerable pressure had been exerted by Grey, the allies signed the Peace Treaty of London. The settlement confirmed the loss by Turkey of all European territory west of a line from Enos to Midia; during the fighting Adrianople had fallen to Bulgaria, and Janina to Greece. Now Europe was faced with the prospect of further hostilities between the former allies, Serbia and Greece, on the one hand, and Bulgaria on the other, who were quarrelling over the division of Macedonia. Grey could only counsel nonintervention by the Great Powers if hostilities broke out again. On the night of 29 June 1913 the Bulgarian army attacked Serbian and Greek positions in Macedonia. The Bulgarians had overestimated their strength and were soon in headlong retreat. To make matters worse Roumania, after King Ferdinand had refused to cede her a large portion of the Dobrudja in the North as a price for her continued neutrality, also declared war on Bulgaria. She was joined by Turkey, anxious to take the opportunity to recapture Adrianople.

Bulgaria's defeat was not regarded with much sorrow by Sazonov. He had long been anxious about the growth of an overpowerful Bulgaria, pro-Austrian in sympathy and with designs on Constantinople. He planned to intervene only if Serbia was crushingly defeated, or if Austria came to the assistance of Bulgaria. Neither of these contingencies materialized—Berchtold, who had meditated intervention, drew back when Austria's ally,

Roumania, entered the fighting. However, a new crisis arose when, on 22 July, Turkey recaptured Adrianople from Bulgaria. Sazonov, despite his antipathy for Bulgaria, declared that Russia could not allow Christians to be restored to Moslem rule. He urged that coercive measures should be taken by the Concert to force Turkey to evacuate the city, and when this was rejected he proposed a Triple Entente naval demonstration at Constantinople. This was in turn rejected by Grey, and the Russian Foreign Minister threatened separate Russian action, either at the Turkish capital or in Armenia, to force the Turks to give way. England, Germany and France were not prepared to take any action that might alienate Turkey: they all feared that separate Russian measures might lead to the collapse of Turkey-in-Asia. Lord Crewe commented that 'it would not have been easy for Grey, after driving his queer diplomatic team for so long and with such success, to drop the reins at the last moment, but luckily Germany, anxious, one may suppose, to revive the greatly cooled affections of the Turks, has declined any joint proceedings.'[36] When France told Russia that separate Russian action might imperil the Triple Entente, Sazonov climbed down, and proposed instead financial sanctions, which were equally unacceptable to his two partners. In the event Turkey remained in possession of Adrianople.

On 30 July 1913 a much chastened Bulgaria concluded an armistice, and on 7 August she signed the Treaty of Bucharest, which formally confirmed her loss to Serbia and Greece of much of the territory in Macedonia for which she had previously fought so hard against Turkey. She was also forced to cede Silistria and the Dobrudja to Roumania. The Great Powers, each fearing for its influence with one or other of the belligerents, decided to accept the *fait accompli*. The labours of the Ambassadorial conference were also coming to an end at this time: Grey decided that they had outlived their usefulness.[37]

Grey had done well during these 'protracted and sometimes intolerably wearisome'[38] negotiations. The Concert of Europe, never a particularly harmonious or united instrument to promote peaceful change, had enjoyed a brief, if frail, renaissance under his leadership. His efforts had contributed to the maintenance of European peace during the crisis, as his contemporaries recognized, and as a result his reputation soared. On 8 January 1913 the

Cabinet paid him a rare courtesy: 'Sir E. Grey was warmly complimented by his colleagues on the skill and success with which he is piloting the European ship through troubled waters.'[39] The King was equally appreciative. Tyrrell wrote of his 'great skill and patience'.[40] Hardinge thought that Grey had established himself 'as a great Foreign Secretary, and what surprised me most, as a strong one'; while Nicolson commented that he 'has shown gifts which I confess I did not think he possessed'.[41]

Anglo-German Relations, 1912–14

Grey ascribed much of his success to what he thought was the willingness of Germany to co-operate with England to secure that the Balkan wars did not involve the Great Powers. He was encouraged in his cautious efforts to improve Anglo-German relations when Gottlieb von Jagow, who became German Foreign Minister in January 1913,[42] suggested that the two countries should press on with their efforts to clear up their misunderstandings. Nevertheless, Grey would not go too far or too fast in this course: he remained at heart suspicious of Germany. Thus he wrote in November 1912:

> At present the Germans seem to desire peace and not to be making mischief. If they could always stick to this line we should get on very well. But I doubt whether good relations between the two Governments have much effect on public opinion in Germany.[43]

At the same time he insisted that England must retain her naval supremacy, for, as he wrote in January 1913, 'the Prussian mentality is such that to be on really good terms with it one must be able to deal with it as equal'.[44]

Nevertheless, relations did improve during the ensuing months. This process was assisted by the success of a visit by the King to Berlin in May 1913 to attend the wedding of the Duke of Cumberland's son to the German Emperor's daughter. The Russian Emperor also attended. The monarchs found themselves in a large measure of agreement over the Balkans; William II outlined to Stamfordham his plans for future Anglo-German co-operation in Turkey and described British fears of a German attack on England as 'the d——dest nonsense he ever heard of'. Nevertheless, the Emperor was disappointed that, in a war between the

Slav races and Austria and Germany, England would probably join Russia and France against 'Anglo-Saxons and Culture'. Later Stamfordham talked with Jagow, who likewise extolled the need for good Anglo-German relations, described a war with the Slavs as inevitable, and dismissed France as 'a decadent Country'.[45] Grey's officials were very worried about the possible consequences of these developments for Britain's future continental relationships. Nicolson thought that

> so long as we maintain unimpaired the present grouping of the Powers a wholesome restraint will be exercised on Germany and it is the best means of preserving European peace. I feel quite convinced that were Germany to know that we should remain neutral in the event of a European War, she would adopt a very different attitude towards France that would compel the latter either to submit to a serious humiliation or to fight it out in desperation.[46]

Others perceived a more sinister influence behind Grey's apparent readiness to coquette with Germany—that of Sir William Tyrrell, Grey's private secretary. According to Valentine Chirol, Tyrrell thought that after her success in localizing the Balkan Wars, England could afford to adopt a more independent attitude towards Russia, whose excesses in Persia and Central Asia filled him with disgust, and that Grey should now go further in promoting an Anglo-German reconciliation. Hardinge was alarmed by these reports.[47] He well knew Tyrrell's influence with Grey, 'who is temperamentally ready to listen to German blandishments, influenced as he is by Haldane in his views'.[48]

Sir Francis Bertie also became impatient with Russia's Balkan policy, and was equally irritated by her behaviour in Persia. He was assiduous during 1913 and 1914 in urging his superiors that neither England nor France should allow themselves to be dragged into war for the sake of Russia's Balkan ambitions. He, like Tyrrell, complained of Nicolson's excessive Russophilia—he once complained that 'in Sir A. Nicolson's view Russia can do no wrong'.[49] Thus there was a growing divergence in the Office between the views on foreign policy of Nicolson and Crowe on the one hand, who continued to believe that Germany could not be trusted, and of Tyrrell and Grey, on the other, who favoured a more flexible British policy. By 1914 it was thought that Nicolson was in total opposition to the Government's policy in Ulster, and that, as a result, Grey had lost all confidence in him; whereas Tyrrell was 'high in favour and everything to Grey'.[50]

There is probably some truth in these accounts of developments in the Foreign Office after 1912, and certainly the descriptions of the bickering and confusion that prevailed there give a gloomy picture of the state of its administration on the eve of the war.[51] Nevertheless, some reservations must be made. Grey and Nicolson did differ on the policy England should adopt towards Europe. Nor can there be any reason to doubt that Grey and his secretary were in agreement about the need to improve Anglo-German relations. However, Grey's move towards Germany was more apparent than real. Grey was determined to preserve the Ententes as an insurance in case Germany's professions of friendship turned out to be fraudulent. His basic distrust of Germany was unimpaired. Nicolson's alternative—that of alliances with France and Russia in order to deter Germany from aggression in the future—was totally unrealistic. Not only might it encourage France and Russia to provoke Germany, secure in the knowledge of British support, but the Cabinet would not have accepted it, as Nicolson himself recognized. Of course Grey's policy did bear all the hallmarks of a compromise between his own convictions and the pressures of his Cabinet colleagues and his critics in the Liberal Party. He firmly believed that for her own safety England would have to come to the aid of France if the latter was attacked by Germany—indeed this was the logic of the military and naval conversations and of practically all British defence preparations since 1906. At the same time he was forced to maintain publicly (and with considerable justification), that England was not in any way obligated to France and Russia in the event of war. His officials feared that France and Russia might take his protestations as evidence that England could not be relied upon in any event, thus impelling them into the arms of Germany. In fact Grey hoped that British public opinion would see that the country's best interests lay in joining France in the event of war, but he made little effort to try to educate the public to an awareness of the issues at stake—and of course he felt that he could not do so since this would lead to a major quarrel with the Cabinet pro-Germans.[52]

His policy was likely to fall between two stools—too friendly towards Germany to please those like Nicolson and Crowe who distrusted her absolutely, and who feared that Germany might, as a result, gamble on British neutrality; and yet, on the other hand, still too pro-French to satisfy the Cabinet pro-Germans. Of these Harcourt remained thoroughly suspicious of the sincerity of Grey's commitment to the new course of Anglo-German friendship. Thus, in January 1914 the Colonial Secretary complained bitterly to Grey about the continued use in despatches of the term 'Triple Entente', 'this terminological inexactitude', 'this mischievous and misleading phrase'. He demanded that it be made absolutely clear to France and Russia that they could expect no help from England in the event of war. 'If the present state of misapprehension is allowed to continue the time is not far distant when we shall be denounced with some truth as "Perfide Albion".' In his reply Grey re-emphasized his adherence to a policy of *détente* with Germany and denied that any misapprehension existed in Europe as to England's overseas obligations:

> The best course I think is to let things go on as they are without any new declaration of policy. The alternatives are either a policy of complete isolation in Europe, or a policy of definite alliance with one or the other group of European Powers. My own desire has been to avoid bringing the choice between these two alternatives to an issue; and I think we have been fortunate in being able to go on so long as we are.

Harcourt abandoned his protests when Grey threatened to take the matter to the Cabinet—Grey's reputation was unassailable by this time, and in any case the Cabinet was too preoccupied by Ulster and the naval estimates to concern itself overmuch with foreign affairs.[53]

The Anglo-German *rapprochement* was bound to rest on insecure foundations when what had been to Grey the real cause of Anglo-German hostility, the naval rivalry between the two countries, remained unsettled. Churchill noted in February 1913 that 'the German fleet development is proceeding with all speed according to the New Law'.[54] However, the heat was taken out of the dispute to some extent when Germany, after 1912, concentrated on increasing the size of her army. Her insecurity became more marked after the Balkan Wars as France was increasing in self-confidence, Russia appeared to be growing in strength, Austria was growing weaker and Italy remained unreliable. The propaganda which accompanied the introduction of the German Army Bill into the Reichstag in January 1913 stressed the danger to Germany of increasing chauvinism in France: as a result Franco-German relations worsened, and the arms race became even more frenzied as France and Russia also increased the size of their armed forces. Even Tirpitz now recognized that Germany could not afford simultaneous increases in her Navy.[55]

There were no further Anglo-German naval talks after 1912. Grey had no wish to be dragged into more fruitless discussions about neutrality formulae, and in any case both Lichnowsky and the German Emperor made it clear that they would resent fresh approaches by England on the naval question. However, Tirpitz, anxious to encourage England to follow Germany in retarding her naval construction, suggested to the Reichstag Budget Committee in February 1913 that England accept a 16 : 10 ratio in dreadnoughts between the two countries.[56] Grey was in a quandary. He had no wish to raise the question since to do so might lead to a worsening of relations between the two countries. His fears were confirmed when, in March 1913, in introducing the naval estimates in the Commons, Churchill rejected Tirpitz's ratio suggestion, and proposed instead a 'naval holiday'—a complete cessation of battleship construction by both countries for one year.[57] The suggestion was received with scant enthusiasm in the German press, and prompted renewed German appeals to Grey that the subject should not be alluded to again. He agreed; but his difficulties were further increased when Bethmann Hollweg told the Reichstag on 7 April 1913 that Germany still awaited concrete naval proposals from England. Churchill protested both to Grey and Asquith that the ban on further references to his proposal would leave him in an invidious position. If the British Government ignored the Chancellor's remarks, radical opinion in England would blame the Liberal Administration for the failure of the two countries to reach a naval agreement. Grey reluctantly conceded that Churchill had a good case, and on 18 October, the First Lord, in a speech at Manchester, repeated his proposal for a naval holiday. According to Goschen, it was received in Germany with 'almost universal disapproval'.[58] Grey thought that 'there was no choice but to say something to our own people about naval expenditure. The Continental response is very bad, but that cannot be helped: the question is a vital one to us, and our people must know where they stand and why. It must be pretty clear to them now.'[59] Consequently Churchill decided to press forward with his plans for increased naval estimates for the following year. He demanded four extra dreadnoughts to take account of continued German building under the 1912 programme, and to replace three dreadnoughts which Canada had promised to build in 1911 but which had subsequently been rejected by the Canadian Senate.[60] His proposals were immediately attacked as over-extravagant by Lloyd George, who mustered a formidable array of supporters in the Cabinet for his position.[61]

The Chancellor protested that the First Lord's additions would result in a dreadnought fleet far in excess of the required sixty per cent superiority over Germany,[62] and he claimed that only two extra dreadnoughts were necessary. Furthermore, he thought that:

> It would be construed as a direct challenge to Germany, and such a policy, at a time when our relations with that country are better than they have been for years, is to say the least of it, highly inopportune.[63]

Churchill retorted that the fate of the British Empire entirely depended on its naval strength, since Britain was a satiated Power who had secured 'an altogether disproportionate share of the wealth and traffic of the world', and there were other non-satiated Powers who resented this fact. Moreover, England could not turn her back on Europe. 'The world is arming as it has never armed before' and even a pacific Liberal Government must face harsh realities.[64]

The quarrel reached serious proportions during January and February 1914. However, early in March 1914, Lloyd George abandoned his opposition and accepted Churchill's proposals in return for a pledge from the latter to reduce expenditure in the following year. The other economists in the Cabinet reluctantly accepted the 'compromise'.[65]

Asquith and Grey adopted a mediatory role throughout; indeed Churchill hinted in December 1913 that he was receiving insufficient support from the Foreign Secretary. No doubt Grey feared that the adoption of an over-large programme by England might lead to fresh pressures in Germany for further increases in the German Navy and to renewed recriminations between the two countries. As it was, both Churchill and Lloyd George made public statements in support of their respective positions which caused uneasiness abroad. In a speech in November 1913 Churchill called for large naval increases, which provoked Lloyd George into an interview with the *Daily Chronicle*, published on 1 January 1914, in which he argued that increased naval estimates were unnecessary in view of the improvement in Anglo-German relations, and because the European Powers were concentrating on military expansion. Grey was reported to be 'furious' about the Chancellor's remarks, which caused considerable uneasiness in France and Russia. It is probable, however, that Grey was annoyed, not with Lloyd George's initiative itself, but because the Chancellor had failed to consult him first about the interview.

Evidence reaching the Foreign Office that the Germans were trying to take advantage of the divisions within the British Cabinet, which had been so publicly revealed, seemed to be substantiated when, early in February 1914, Tirpitz, in rejecting once again the idea of a naval holiday, told the Reichstag Budget Committee that he was prepared to consider accepting a ratio of 5 German dreadnoughts squadron to 8 British as the future German standard. Grey now felt that he must make some response. In a speech at Manchester on 3 February 1914 he reminded his audience that British suggestions for multilateral reductions in armaments had not been well received in the past. Under these circumstances 'it is felt by us that we must wait until other great Countries in Europe are penetrated with the same feelings as we ourselves have with regard to arresting the expenditure on armaments'.[66] There the matter rested. There were no further naval proposals before the outbreak of war.[67]

The Anglo-German negotiations about the Portuguese colonies[68] continued during 1913. Nicolson described the eventual agreement as 'one of the most cynical diplomatic acts in my memory', while Hardinge could not understand how 'a loyal and straight person' like Grey could ever have agreed to it.[69]

While Grey persisted for a time with his scheme to make the Anglo-Portuguese alliance terminable—he dismissed his officials' complaints with the retort that, 'British opinion will not tolerate active defence of scandals by an alliance'[70]—both he and Harcourt eventually decided to drop the idea on the ground that the strategic risks were too great. Throughout the negotiations with Germany, Grey's officials referred to German efforts to introduce clauses providing for German interference in the spheres allotted to her, in case of Portuguese misrule, or the continuation of slavery, as crude devices to secure the colonies in advance of any financial difficulties, and to deprive England of the right to protest. They warned Grey that the inclusion of the islands of St Thomé and Principé in the German sphere would affect French interests in Central Africa, and that a clause providing for Anglo-German co-operation to exclude the political and economic interference of third Powers in the Portuguese colonies, would certainly offend France. The negotiations were concluded by the end of August 1913. The provisions for the coming into operation of the treaty were not markedly different from those of the 1898 agreement,[71] except that England now secured a larger portion of South Mozambique as her sphere, but abandoned most of Angola to Germany, except for a small strip on the frontier of Northern Rhodesia. Neither Power was to support concessions by its nationals in the sphere assigned to the other.[72]

Throughout, Grey faced an awkward dilemma—anxious to improve Anglo-German relations, yet, on the other hand, uneasily aware that the agreement conflicted with England's obligations to Portugal. He therefore insisted, both to Harcourt, who was anxious for the speedy signature of the convention, and to the Germans, not only on the publication of the 1898 and 1913 agreements with Germany, but also on the simultaneous publication of the 1899 treaty with Portugal, in order to demonstrate to Portugal England's continued commitment to her defence. Bethmann protested that the German people would deride the conclusion of an Anglo-German agreement which could not be put into operation owing to England's obligations to defend Portugal and her Empire. Bertie noted in February 1914:

> Crowe informed me that Harcourt had been commissioned by Grey to have a give and take negotiation with the German Embassy, but that Harcourt had told the Under Secretary at the Colonial Office, Sir J. Anderson, that for political reasons he wanted to make concessions to Germany and Anderson was therefore to devise a scheme which would do so and have only an appearance of giving satisfaction to our interests. The result of Harcourt's negotiation is the

initialled arrangements which Grey *now* wishes to render abortive, and by which we get next to nothing.[73]

Certainly Grey was encountering serious complications by 1914. Rumours of the revised agreement were provoking angry protests from France and Portugal. The French complained about the secrecy with which the negotiations had been conducted, and the damaging effects some of its provisions would have on her colonial interests. Bertie warned his superiors that its publication would cause an 'explosion' in France against the Entente, and he appealed to Grey to 'avoid a publication, or will the German Government make the arrangements known in order to create a sore between France and England?'[74]

It was obvious, too, that Germany was anxious to lay her hands on the colonies as soon as possible. Grey noted Lichnowsky's dissatisfaction when he tried to emphasize that the agreement would enable Portugal to develop her colonies with the aid of Anglo-German capital, and that they should not be taken away from her without her consent.[75] Sir Arthur Hardinge commented in October 1913 that 'the Germans are watching this poor country's gradual ruin much as a vulture with half shut eyes blinks at a dying antelope in the African bush'.[76]

In these circumstances Grey seized gratefully on a suggestion by Lichnowsky on 3 March 1914 that, in view of the publication difficulties, the agreement should be abandoned for the time being. This was not, however, Germany's last word on the subject. Jagow and Lichnowsky continued to press for the signature of the agreement in advance of publication. Grey refused, pointing to the opposition of Parliament to secret agreements. He promised he would make no new agreement with Portugal or third Powers about the colonies without consulting Germany first. This seemed to satisfy Jagow, who added ominously that

> he hoped, however, that soon, namely, when German colonial territory reached larger dimensions and when consequently public attention on colonial matters would be extended over a larger field, the Imperial Government would be in a position to raise no objections to the publication of both Treaties. In the meantime the Imperial Government considered themselves morally bound by the initialled agreement.[77]

These remarks excited considerable speculation in the Foreign Office. It was pointed out that whereas England still regarded the 1898 agreement as in operation until the 1913 agreement was signed, Germany evidently thought otherwise. However, to avoid 'a rather embarrassing discussion', Grey decided to accept Jagow's word as applying to his (Grey's) pledge not to make a new agreement with third Powers without consulting Germany. The confusion became worse when the German Government began to support applications by its nationals for concessions in areas assigned to Germany in the 1913 agreement, but to England in that of 1898.[78] While Crowe pressed for a declaration to Germany that England did not accept the 1913 agreement, Harcourt, in April, urged Grey that, in view of the prevailing uncertainty, the British Government ought to decide on the future of the agreements without delay. The war ended further speculation.[79]

England, the Near East and Turkey to 1914

A year of uneasy peace followed the end of the Balkan Wars in the summer of 1913. As Nicolson put it with characteristic gloom in October:

> The fact of the matter is that peace has only been patched up and we have still many questions unsettled. The Conferences of the Ambassadors were certainly of use in as far as they kept the Powers together and prevented any serious friction arising between them. It can hardly be said however that the questions with which the Powers had to deal have been definitely and satisfactorily settled. ... I expect that before many years have elapsed we shall find South-Eastern Europe plunged once again into the turmoil of hostilities.[80]

Austro-Russian and Austro-Serbian relations were extremely hostile, Bulgaria was seeking an opportunity to revenge herself on her former allies, while Turkey threatened to go to war with Greece to recover some of the Aegean Islands which Greece had occupied during the Balkan Wars. Grey's efforts to find a settlement of this question merely offended both countries. Italy failed to evacuate the Dodecanese Islands despite frequent promises to do so—Nicolson commented that 'I do not think that Italy ever plays a straight game or that much reliance can be placed upon her word.'[81]

Albania was another area of instability. Nicolson doubted 'that this somewhat artificial creation will have a very long life', and he forecast its collapse in the future, followed by its partition between Austria and Italy.[82] 'The whole of this Albanian question seems to me such a fiction and unreality that I really cannot take any intense interest in it, especially as what occurs in that part of the world is of very little concern to us, and we have no interest whatever there.'[83] Austria, however, remained intensely interested in the country. When Serbia occupied border territory in Northern Albania, Austria ordered her to withdraw without delay on 18 October 1913. Serbia complied, much to Grey's relief. Albania remained in a disordered and unsettled condition down to the outbreak of the first world war.

In Turkey, England struggled to retain some vestiges of her former influence in the face of what seemed to the Foreign Office to be increasing German predominance in the counsels of the Young Turks.[84] Grey inaugurated a new British effort to revive Anglo-Turkish friendship, when, in December 1913, he replaced Lowther by Sir Louis Mallet. Grey was 'very conscious in these last five years that I have made several mistakes about Constantinople things and anyone in Lowther's place might justly say that he hasn't had very much help: but that doesn't alter the necessity in the public interest for a change.'[85]

From the start Mallet's efforts were frustrated by Russia's hostility towards Turkey and her opposition to British attempts to encourage Turkey's regeneration. He believed that 'if the Triple Entente worked together on the lines of preserving Turkey's integrity and improving her administration we could do a great deal and easily obtain a preponderating influence'.[86] Russia however appeared uninterested in the survival of Turkey-in-Asia, and seemed only to be waiting the chance to secure Constantinople and Armenia. England, Germany and France, on the other hand, had important economic interests in Turkey which might be seriously affected by the collapse of the Empire: moreover its disintegration would lead to a scramble for territory by the Great Powers which might result in serious complications. British interests in the event of a Turkish collapse were clear. As Lord Crewe remarked: 'If the present wretched Government which is no improvement on that of Abdul Hamid, breaks up in flame and massacre . . . we must have a free hand, only saying to everybody "Hands off" Aden and the Persian Gulf.'[87] The British however hoped to postpone the evil day by a renewed effort to persuade Turkey to introduce reforms in the Empire and to satisfy the grievances of minorities, like the Armenians, who might otherwise revolt. Asquith was somewhat dubious about the prospects for this policy. He reported to the King on 10 July that:

> Sir E. Grey is of the opinion (and so are the Cabinet) that for the time being the only safe policy is to preserve Ottoman rule in Asia. The Prime Minister, while assenting to this view, expressed a strong opinion that it was only a question of time before the same causes of instability and rottenness which have led to the practical expulsion of the Turks from Europe would bring about the same downfall in Asia, and that we ought to face these probabilities.[88]

However, Grey persisted with his efforts, although these were largely frustrated by his inability to interest British capitalists in developing Turkish trade and finance,[89] and his unwillingness to go too far in helping them 'in the sense of having rows with other Powers on their behalf'.[90]

He soon faced a quarrel with Russia over his willingness in 1913 to meet a Turkish request to provide British officers to organize a gendarmerie in Armenia. Russia demanded the right to supply Russian officers in a province which bordered her Empire, and would not accept the employment of British officers there. Turkey would not agree to ask for Russian assistance: as a Young Turk told Sir Henry Wilson in October 1913, 'he would prefer going to hell in his own way than to Paradise under the tutelage of Russia'.[91] Sazonov warned Grey that if Turkey failed to introduce genuine reforms in Armenia, and massacres ensued, Russia would be forced to intervene. The Foreign Office feared that he was preparing the ground for a Russian occupation of Armenia. The Russian Foreign Minister proposed a reform scheme which, Grey complained, would practically make Armenia a Russian sphere of influence, and might presage the partition of the Empire. The Turks rejected the scheme and put forward one of their own, which was in turn rejected by Russia. The Foreign Office was divided over the policy which England should adopt in Turkey. While Mallet recommended Anglo-German co-operation to secure a workable reform programme, Nicolson urged full co-operation with Russia and suspected that the whole thing was a Turco-German plot to create dissension between Russia and England.

By the outbreak of the war little or nothing had been done in the way of Turkish reforms. It was evident that the Turks would only accept a workable programme under duress, and to this England and Germany were totally opposed. No British officers were sent to Armenia, and thus, through his anxiety to reconcile the diametrically opposed attitudes of Turkey and Russia, Grey had lost what Mallet had envisaged as a valuable opportunity to increase British influence in the Ottoman dominions.

A new crisis arose when Turkey, in an effort to improve the efficiency of her army after the Balkan *débâcle*, secured the appointment of a strong German military mission to Constantinople, led by a General Liman von Sanders. Sazonov was beside himself with fury when he discovered that Liman would have command of the Turkish Army Corps in Constantinople. He suspected a German attempt to gain control of the Straits, and he pointed out that Liman would have a crucial political role in the capital, especially in times of unrest.

He threatened Russian action to secure equivalent privileges elsewhere in the Empire. When Grey warned him that this might lead to the collapse of Turkey, he demanded Anglo-French co-operation to secure the termination of the appointment: it would be, he said, 'a test of the value of [the] Triple *Entente*'.[92] Grey was in an invidious position. He thought that Sazonov was exaggerating the importance of the appointment which, in any case, hardly affected British interests. Besides, a British Admiral was engaged in reforming the Turkish navy, which he commanded in peace time. A British fuss about the German General might provoke a German fuss about the British Admiral: with the disappearance of the Admiral might go the contracts for arsenal supplies and dock building monopolies held by British firms—'about our only asset in this country', according to Mallet.[93] Furthermore, English protests about the appointment at Berlin and Constantinople might destroy the Anglo-German *détente* and wreck Grey's efforts to improve relations with the Porte. If Germany insisted on the appointment, the issue might broaden into a serious confrontation between Germany and Turkey on the one hand, and Russia on the other.

Yet if Grey failed to give some support to Russia, the Entente might be placed in jeopardy. Grey did not 'believe the thing is worth all the fuss that Sazonov makes about it: but as long as he does make a fuss it will be important and very embarrassing to us: for we can't turn our back on Russia.'[94] He worked to prevent the question becoming a serious issue between the Triple Entente and the Triple Alliance, and by the exercise of patient pressure at Berlin, persuaded the Germans to agree, in January 1914, to a compromise solution whereby Liman was promoted to the rank of Marshal in the Turkish Army, and relinquished his command of the Turkish Army Corps.

The Baghdad Railway and the Gulf

The Baghdad Railway negotiations with Turkey moved closer towards a settlement in July 1912, when Grey decided to abandon his efforts to secure a majority of shares for the Triple Entente in the Gulf section of the line. Grey now offered to withdraw his demand for British participation in the railway, provided that it terminated at Basra, and that no attempt would be made to extend it to the Gulf without prior agreement with England.[95] He further required that Turkey should prohibit differential rates on all her Asiatic railways (i.e. British goods should not pay higher tariffs than those of other nations); that two British directors should be appointed to the Board of the Baghdad Railway Company to ensure equality of treatment; and that the Turks should recognize the independence of Bahrain, Muscat, El Katr and various Gulf Islands, and recognize England's exclusive right to police the Persian Gulf. Other British requirements included the extension of the British shipping monopoly on the Tigris-Euphrates rivers, certain conditions about the navigation of the Shatt-El-Arab, and the renunciation by Turkey of her veto on Egypt's borrowing powers. In return Britain would recognize Turkey's sovereignty over an autonomous Kuwait, and agree to the three per cent increase in Turkey's customs. Thus Britain was now concentrating almost entirely on the protection of her position on the Gulf—indeed in 1913 she rejected a German application to establish a cable station there. Provided that Britain's commercial interests in Mesopotamia were protected, Grey now decided that he was indifferent as to who built the Baghdad-Basra line.

Much of the detailed negotiations were carried out between Hakki Pasha, a special Turkish negotiator, who arrived in London early in 1913, and Alwyn Parker of the Foreign Office. By the end of August 1913, England had secured the bulk of her demands. Parallel negotiations were also in progress with the Germans, who were now as anxious as the British to resolve this tiresome question. By the summer of 1913 Kühlmann agreed that a new German company would construct the Baghdad-Basra line, that the Gulf section would be postponed, and that it would be constructed in the future only with the prior agreement of England, Turkey and Germany. The German company would claim only a share of the construction, but no part of the management of the Gulf line, and would renounce its right to build the Gulf terminus. Two British directors were to be appointed to the Baghdad-Basra Railway Board. British interests were to secure forty per cent of the construction of the ports at Basra and Baghdad. England would support the completion of the Baghdad Railway as far as Basra, and would not support applications by her nationals for competing lines between Konia and Basra.

These agreements had to wait the conclusion of similar negotiations between France and Germany, Turkey and Germany, and the Baghdad Railway Company and Turkey. There were also difficulties about the Shatt-El-Arab navigation, the British-owned Smyrna-Aidin Railway, and the British shipping monopoly on the Tigris and Euphrates, which were not ironed out until 1914. In addition there was a complicated series of negotiations concerning oil concessions in the Turkish Empire. The issue had long caused contention between England and Germany. A British company, the Anglo-Persian Oil Company, and a German company, the Turkish Petroleum Company, which was owned by the Baghdad Railway, both claimed somewhat shadowy Turkish concessions to drill for oil in the Turkish Empire, particularly in Mesopotamia. The Turkish Government, faced with the rivalry of Germany and England, each supporting its own claimant, had failed to confirm either concession down to 1913. However, with the improvement in Anglo-German relations in 1913, the two sides agreed to merge their interests in a new joint company. The agreement was finalized on a 50 : 50 basis at the Foreign Office on 19 March 1914, although Grey had to apply persistent pressure on the Turks before they would agree to award the lease of the Mesopotamian oil wells to the company in June.[96]

The Anglo-German railway convention was finally initialled on

15 June 1914. Grey had achieved a settlement that had eluded Lansdowne in 1902, although of course the Baghdad Railway remained an all-German concern, which had been far from Lansdowne's intention. But at least Grey had secured formal Turkish recognition of England's strategic and political monopoly on the Persian Gulf, although even here her commercial predominance was being steadily eroded by growing German competition.

Anglo-Russian Relations

Between 1912 and 1914 relations between England and Russia were more strained than at any time since 1907. The two countries were squabbling about the future of Turkey, and Russia complained that she was receiving little British support in southeastern Europe. The Russians also regarded with increasing suspicion Grey's willingness to collaborate with Germany in the Balkans, Turkey and in Africa. In the Foreign Office only Nicolson remained a staunch supporter of the Entente with Russia, willing, according to Bertie, to sacrifice all other considerations to the maintenance of the agreement. The Permanent Under-Secretary feared that Russia would soon become alienated by England's lukewarm attitude to the Entente and that, as a result, she might turn to Germany, with devastating consequences for England's security in the Near and Middle East. Grey, Bertie and Tyrrell were all, in varying degrees, as critical of Nicolson's pro-Russian sympathies, as they were of Russia's shortcomings in the Balkans and in Persia.

Persia was the greatest obstacle to the maintenance of good relations between England and Russia. By the end of 1912 conditions there had gone from bad to worse. The Persian Government would not accept Russia's nominee, Sa'ad ud Dowla, as Regent, nor was he able to form a government of his own at Tehran. As a result Russia saw the disappearance of her last hope of establishing a more sympathetic régime in Persia. Indeed the Central Government remained implacably hostile to Russia, and with good reason. Consequently, the Russians concentrated on consolidating and extending their political, strategic, and commercial interests in North Persia, with disastrous consequences both for Persia's stability and for Grey's peace of mind.

On 14 May 1913, wearying of continual British complaints

about Russian interference in the north, Sazonov suggested a revision of the 1907 agreement to allow Russia to secure a freer hand in the north, and Britain the bulk (but not all) of the neutral sphere. Grey and Crewe remained opposed to any further moves towards the *de facto* partition of Persia. Not only did they fear an explosion of wrath from their Liberal supporters, and possible complications with the other European Powers, but also neither they nor the Government of India wanted to increase Britain's responsibilities in Persia.

Nicolson and Buchanan, on the other hand, while recognizing the difficulties, favoured a settlement of all the problems facing Russia and England in Persia and in Central Asia. They believed that, since the two countries were demonstrably unable to co-operate to uphold the Persian Government, they should now recognize the fact, and agree to partition the country. They pointed out that, in any case, as a result of Russian advances in China, a decision about the future distribution of the entire area could not be indefinitely postponed.

Russia had taken advantage of the confusion prevailing in the new Chinese Republic to reach agreement with Peking in November 1913, whereby Russia recognized Chinese suzerainty over an autonomous Outer Mongolia in return for a promise that China would not send troops into the country, or intervene in its internal affairs. Other ominous portents of Russian expansionism in Central Asia included the conclusion of a mutual assistance agreement between Outer Mongolia and Tibet in January 1913, an instrument which, the Foreign Office feared, would enable Russia to utilize her hold on Outer Mongolia to interfere in Tibetan affairs. Furthermore, should the Chinese province of Sinkiang also become a virtual Russian protectorate, there would no longer be a neutral barrier between Outer Mongolia and Tibet. Hardinge watched these developments with mounting concern. He still wanted compensation for India in Tibet to offset the changes which had taken place in Central Asia in Russia's favour, and pressed London to agree to the establishment of a British agent in Lhasa, and for an Anglo-Chinese agreement on Tibet similar to that between Russia and China on Mongolia. Otherwise he was apprehensive that the Dalai Lama, fearful of renewed Chinese efforts to re-establish their sovereignty over his land, might turn to Russia for advice and assistance.[97]

Grey and Crewe would not hear of an approach to Sazonov on these lines. Sazonov had made it clear at Balmoral that he would not agree to an Outer Mongolia-Tibet deal, and had hinted that if England wanted changes in her favour in Tibet, Russia would demand that she should establish direct relations with Afghanistan.[98] Crewe, while he sympathized with Hardinge's views, warned the Viceroy that the Cabinet would not agree to a renegotiation and an enlargement of the 1907 Convention with Russia, while Morley would 'have a fit' if India asked to send an agent to Lhasa.[99] As a result of this opposition from London, Hardinge fell back on a more roundabout strategy to secure his ends in Tibet—to persuade China and Tibet to reach an agreement whereby China accept a purely nominal sovereignty over Tibet. Accordingly Chinese and Tibetan representatives were invited to India in 1913 to discuss a new Sino-Tibetan treaty. The Indian Foreign Minister, Sir Henry McMahon, was to act as 'an honest broker' in these negotiations.[100]

Meanwhile events in Persia were moving towards an acute crisis. Russian consuls were behaving like rulers in the North—seizing control of the provincial finances from Central Government agencies, preventing the Swedish-led gendarmerie from operating there, collecting taxes directly from Russian subjects, allowing Russian subjects to buy land in the North in defiance of Russia's treaty obligations, and interfering with the provincial administration. Sazonov refused to withdraw Russian forces, who numbered about 17,000 in 1913, from the North. The Tehran Government was helpless to resist the steady Russian penetration of its northern provinces. Grey's protests merely offended Sazonov without leading to any amelioration of the situation. In May 1914 Buchanan declared that 'the greater part of North Persia is already Russian in all but name'.[101]

The British were even more alarmed when Russia began to extend her influence into the province of Isfahan in the neutral zone, with the object of sealing off the North altogether from British trade, and creating a monopoly there for Russian commerce. The British responded by urging their traders to make great efforts to maintain Britain's commercial preponderance in the neutral zone. The neutral zone had assumed a greater importance in British eyes by 1914 as a result of the discovery of huge oil deposits there. In February 1914 Churchill persuaded the

Cabinet to purchase a controlling Government interest in the Anglo-Persian Oil Company, a British concern. The Navy was gradually switching from coal to oil fuel, and the Admiralty believed that in the Anglo-Persian Oil Company's Persian concessions it had found a safe and reliable source. It was argued that Southern Persia could be easily defended from the sea, that the company was already working several wells in the South, and that the injection of Government capital would enable it to develop new fields in the neutral zone without having to resort to foreign, perhaps even German, finance. The Admiralty negotiated bulk long-term contracts with the company, and estimated that, as a result, it had secured a cheap and reliable supply of oil for its ships.[102]

However, the arrangement led to serious complications with the Russian Government. By the terms of a concession obtained from the Persian Government in 1901, the company claimed the right to drill for oil throughout Persia. Grey believed that the concession was still valid since it antedated the 1907 convention. Sazonov contended that the situation was altered by the British Government's purchase of the company's shares, and demanded that the company renounce the right to drill for oil in the North. The Russians had further grievances against the British. No progress had been made in selecting a route for a railway line across Persia from Russia to India, a project which Russia had been pressing since 1907. The Government of India and the military members of the Committee of Imperial Defence were acutely suspicious of the motives of the Russian Government in promoting the scheme which, they claimed, would threaten Indian security. Sazonov protested frequently about England's obstructive tactics towards the projected railway, but there was little Grey could do to persuade the Indian Government to agree to its construction.[103]

By the spring and summer of 1914 Anglo-Russian differences in Persia and Central Asia were coming to a head. On 27 April 1914 McMahon persuaded the Chinese and Tibetan representatives to initial the Simla Convention, whereby China agreed not to send troops to, or interfere in, the administration of Central (Outer) Tibet, although her nominal sovereignty over the whole country was recognized by Tibet. In effect Outer Tibet would come under British influence, for the British Government secured the right to mediate Sino-Tibetan differences in future, and to send a trade agent on visits to Lhasa.[104] Buchanan suggested to Sazonov a month later that this agreement, if approved by Russia, would represent a fair price for Russia's advances in North Persia. Sazonov rejected this interpretation, and made it clear that in return for approving the Simla Convention Russia would require counter-concessions, and he put forward a Russian protectorate in Azerbaijan, a commercial outlet for Russia on the Persian Gulf, and the recognition of Herat in North Afghanistan as being in the Russian sphere, as instances of what he had in mind.[105]

Grey would not consider such extensive proposals. He pointed out to Buchanan in March 1914 that although England wanted most of the neutral sphere in Persia and changes in the status of Tibet in her favour, she could not agree, on the other hand, to closer Russo-Afghan relations. 'So all along the line we want something and we have nothing to give. It is therefore difficult to see how a good bargain is to be made . . . For these reasons, I hesitate to propose a general discussion at present, although I realise that events are forcing us nearer to it.'[106]

As Grey wavered about Tibet and Central Asia, Sazonov lost patience, and complained that England had adopted a hostile policy towards Russia in Tibet and Persia, where she was intriguing to acquire the neutral zone. While vigorously denying these assertions, Grey's officials recognized that a serious rift between the two countries was now in prospect, and they urged Grey to propose the partition of Persia to Sazonov as the only solution to the Anglo-Russian difficulties there. After further angry exchanges between Sazonov and Buchanan, during the course of which the Russian said he was 'sick to death' of Grey's continual complaints about North Persia, Grey, on 10 June 1914, drew up a despatch for Buchanan, in which he catalogued the various Russian advances in North Persia and in the neutral zone, and instructed the Ambassador to demand Russian acceptance of the strengthening of England's strategic and political interests in the Gulf and the neutral zone, as compensation for Russia's increased power in the North.

Sazonov's reply disappointed those in the Foreign Office, like Nicolson and Crowe, who had hoped that Grey's despatch would encourage the Russian Foreign Minister to take the bull by the horns and propose the outright partition of Persia between the

two countries, Grey evidently being too concerned about unfavourable Cabinet reactions to suggest such a solution himself.
Sazonov would not agree to the inclusion of the whole of the
neutral zone in the British sphere. He repeated his demand for
concessions for Russia in North Afghanistan.[107] He said that he
would try to control the activities of Russia's consuls in North
Persia, a promise he was evidently unable to fulfil. As a result
Grey could only continue to protest about Russia's excesses in the
North. Even Nicolson felt that 'Russia has gone farther and faster
than she should have done in Persia' and could only conclude that,
'our relations with Russia are now approaching a point where we
shall have to make up our minds as to whether we should become
really intimate and permanent friends, or else diverge into another
path.'[108] The Foreign Office suggested a new British approach to
Russia on the partition of Persia on 21 July 1914, but Grey was
now too taken up by the European crisis to give the matter any
attention.

England, Germany and the Triple Entente, 1914

The difficulty with Russia about Persia was merely another, albeit
more serious, manifestation of the weakness and divisions within
the Triple Entente in the years immediately prior to the outbreak
of the world war. France too was giving the directors of British
foreign policy cause for serious concern. Thus Grey found the
growing spirit of xenophobia in France after 1912 'very unwhole-
some',[109] and he reacted sharply to reports from Bertie that certain
French generals and ultra-patriotic elements were clamouring for
war with Germany as a means of recovering Alsace-Lorraine.
England, Grey wrote, would not support France if she went to
war to recover the Lost Provinces!

> It will not at all be the same thing as it was in 1911 and 1906 when
> it appeared that Germany was inclined to force war upon France.
> We must deprecate, as far as we can, this aggressive spirit in
> France.[110]

While Nicolson agreed that, under these circumstances, British
assistance to France would be impossible, he still felt, somewhat
illogically, that an Anglo-French-Russian alliance was the only
sure guarantee of peace, and the only way of convincing France

and Russia of England's steadfastness. 'It is however, I know, quite out of the question for any Government to take such a step, so I suppose we must continue to drift along in our present uncertain manner.'[111] As Grey and Bertie pointed out, an Anglo-French-Russian alliance would merely encourage the hot-heads in France and Russia, and, in view of the strained relations between France and Germany, and between Russia and Germany in 1914, Bertie believed that the very uncertainty of British aid in war-time made the other two Entente countries more cautious.

Nevertheless, it appeared to many in London, Paris and St Petersburg that some gesture of support for France and Russia ought to be made by England to restore the solidarity of the Triple Entente which, it was avowed by the French and Russian Governments, had been so much weakened by closer Anglo-German relations since 1912. The French evinced great concern about any signs of good Anglo-German relations, and protested when Asquith assured the House of Commons in March 1913 that England was in no way committed to support France, and when both the Prime Minister and Grey made friendly references to Germany in speeches.

Bertie had already, in June 1913, suggested to Grey that he make some vague assurances to France about future Anglo-French co-operation in Europe, but:

> Grey did not think that the Cabinet would consent to go beyond the private letters [between Grey and Cambon in November 1912]. To do so would certainly cause some resignations. To this I answered that the Cabinet contained so many members that some might be spared.[112]

An opportunity to do something in this direction was presented to both Bertie and the French in April 1914, when the King visited Paris to return a visit by Poincaré to London in the previous year. The Foreign Office hoped that the visit would revive the popularity of the Entente in the French mind, and convince the French people that King George was as much a Francophil as King Edward had been. The King was accompanied, with considerable reluctance, by Grey, his first venture overseas since he had become Foreign Secretary.

Bertie suggested to the French that they ask Grey to subscribe to an Anglo-French-Russian declaration pledging mutual consultation in the event of a threat to European peace. Poincaré and

Doumergue, the French Foreign Minister, did not take up Bertie's suggestion when they met Grey on 23 April; but they did raise a proposal which both the Russian Emperor and Sazonov had mentioned on a number of occasions since 1912—that Anglo-Russian naval staff talks should be held to prepare for mutual co-operation in the event of war. While his officials were all in favour of such talks, Grey doubted that they would be of much use, since the British Navy would not try to enter the Baltic in war-time, and the Russian fleet was still a negligible quantity. However, in order not to disappoint the French and Russians, he agreed to raise the matter in the Cabinet, although he emphasized to Doumergue that an alliance with Russia was out of the question owing to the unpopularity of the autocracy in England. The Cabinet, pressed by Churchill, agreed on 13 May, to the opening of naval talks with Russia, although it stressed their non-binding nature.[113]

Unfortunately for Grey the arrangement was leaked to the French press, leading to the inevitable Parliamentary questions, and forcing Grey to phrase his denials in somewhat disingenuous terms.[114] He complained to Bertie on 25 June, while the latter was in London, that the leakage might destroy the Anglo-German *détente*, and lead to a fresh round of naval increases. When Bertie suggested that Germany might be restrained from going to war by the knowledge of closer ties between the members of the Triple Entente, Grey demurred. 'We are on good terms with Germany now,' he replied, 'and we desire to avoid a revival of friction with her, and we wish to discourage the French from provoking Germany.' He hoped for further Anglo-German co-operation in the event of renewed trouble in the Balkans:

I [Bertie] supposed and Grey said correctly that he would continue the intimate conversations and consultations with France and to a lesser degree with Russia and to consult with Germany as far as it may be expedient as to be a connecting link with Germany and the Triple Entente and a restraint on the hastiness of Austria and Italy.[115]

The Germans appeared satisfied by Grey's subsequent denials that England was not obligated in any way to France and Russia, and by his admission that there had been naval and military talks with France in the past but that they in no way affected England's liberty of action in the event of war. He again described England's task as to act as a bridge between the two alliance systems. He expounded further his concept of England's role on the continent in a conversation with Bertie a few weeks before the outbreak of the war. He now believed that Germany was genuinely afraid of the growing strength of the Russian army, and he feared that if her apprehensions were not calmed she would either increase further the size of her army, or launch a preventive war before Russia's programme of military and railway reconstruction was completed.[116] Thus he hoped to continue his work as mediator on the continent, a task for which he thought England was especially suited both on temperamental and geographical grounds.

The Coming of War[117]

The relatively quiet atmosphere prevailing in Europe in the spring and early summer of 1914 appeared to favour the success of Grey's plans for a period of peaceful co-existence between the two alliance groupings. As Nicolson remarked in May: 'since I have been at the Foreign Office I have not seen such calm waters.'[118] Hence the assassination of the heir to the Habsburg throne, Francis Ferdinand, on 28 June 1914, at Sarajevo, did not at first cause the Foreign Office much perturbation.

To most observers Austria-Hungary appeared to be well on the way to disintegration by 1914; indeed many forecast that the death of the aged Emperor, Francis Joseph, would be the signal for the collapse of the multi-national Empire. Francis Ferdinand, however, believed that the Empire could be saved if it were transformed into a federal structure. He intended, on succeeding to the throne, to confer on the Slav nationalities the same degree of self-government as had been secured by the Germans and Hungarians in 1867. Inevitably his plans were strongly opposed by the Hungarians, who were not willing to surrender the monopoly of power which they exercised in their portion of the Empire. The Serbs found it equally unpalatable, since they were only waiting for the collapse of the Empire in order to achieve their dream of the unification of the Slav races within Serbia. They feared that a federal solution might reconcile the nationalities to the Empire, which was of course Francis Ferdinand's motive in propounding the scheme.

Despite frequent promises to desist, the Serbs had continued their irredentist agitation in Austria's troubled provinces of Bosnia-Herzegovina. Since 1911 a number of secret societies had sprung up within Serbia dedicated to achieving a greater Serbia by means both of propaganda and of terrorist methods. Many of these societies had close links with the Serbian army and numerous para-military agencies. The Serbian Government, itself weak and divided, could do nothing to control the activities of these secret societies, which attracted support from all sections of Serbian opinion, including the Royal House. Certain students and army officers planned to assassinate Francis Ferdinand during his visit to Bosnia-Herzegovina to review the troops: the visit to the province was somewhat tactlessly timed to coincide with a Serbian national holiday on 28 June 1914. The Serbian Government was aware of the plot, but the Austrian authorities ignored unofficial Serbian warnings about it. Both the Archduke and his wife were shot dead by a Croatian student, Gavrilo Princip, on the morning of the 28th. Little regret was felt either in the Austrian court or in Hungary about the disappearance of the heir to the throne, who was unpopular, while in Serbia considerable relief was expressed openly in the press about the removal of this exponent of a trialist Habsburg Empire.

The Austrian Government, whose poor security arrangements in Sarajevo had been partially responsible for the assassination, was determined to utilize the opportunity to put an end once and for all to the incessant pinpricks which it had for so long endured from Serbia. In this resolve Austria was fully supported by her German ally, who believed that if Austria did not discipline Serbia, her prestige would be so badly undermined as to render her continued existence as a Great Power highly questionable, and hasten her demise. Thus throughout the ensuing crisis the key to peace lay in Berlin: if the Germans had restrained their ally the incident would have been settled without recourse to war. Unfortunately, for the first time since the alliance of 1878, Germany encouraged Austria to take decisive action, and pledged German military assistance should war ensue. In fact Bethmann Hollweg was confident that hostilities would be avoided and that the Austro-Serbian dispute would be 'localized', as he put it, without the intervention of the Triple Entente. He reasoned that England's recent European policy demonstrated her unwillingness to be drawn into a European War, especially as she was at the same time deeply divided by the Ulster crisis; while he thought that Russia would not intervene since her military preparations were not yet completed. Thus the German Chancellor was confident that the Central Powers could win a cheap diplomatic triumph on the same lines as that of 1909. He failed to understand that Russia could not endure another humiliation and that, if Austria tried to crush Serbia, Russia would have to come to the latter's aid.

On 7 July 1914 the Austro-Hungarian Council of Ministers resolved on the adoption of firm measures against Serbia. Only the Hungarian Prime Minister, Tisza, objected to a policy likely to lead to the addition of more unruly Slavs to the Empire, and which might, at the same time, end in a general war. The strength of his opposition was, however, much weakened by Germany's support for harsh Austrian sanctions against Serbia. Eventually Berchtold overcame Tisza's resistance by promising that Austria would not annex Serbian territory: Tisza hoped that this promise would be sufficient to enable Russia to wash her hands of the dispute.

It took the vacillating Berchtold from 7 to 19 July to formulate the terms of the proposed ultimatum to Serbia, which was to be so worded as to cause its rejection by Serbia, thus paving the way for an Austrian invasion of the country. The Germans evinced increasing impatience with the dilatory behaviour of their ally, and Berchtold was under strong pressure from Berlin to hasten the despatch of the ultimatum to Belgrade.[119]

Grey was blissfully unaware of these undercurrents. Neither he nor Nicolson believed that Austria would take any serious action: even as late as 20 July the latter still hoped 'that matters will not be pushed to an extremity'.[120] While Bethmann concealed the true aims of his policy not only from Grey but also from Lichnowsky, the British Foreign Secretary hoped that should there be further trouble in south-eastern Europe, England and Germany would co-operate, as they had done during the Balkan Wars, to maintain European peace. When Lichnowsky warned Grey on 6 July that Austria was meditating some punitive action against Serbia, Grey promised to 'use all the influence I could to mitigate difficulties and smooth them away'.[121] Thus from the beginning of the crisis Grey adopted the role of mediator, a task which he was gradually and reluctantly forced to abandon.

At last, on 23 July 1914, the Austrian ultimatum was handed to Serbia. It was a rude awakening for Grey. Austria demanded *inter alia* that her police should co-operate with Serbian authorities in suppressing the anti-Austrian nationalist movement within Serbia, and that Serbia should agree to a joint Austro-Serbian investigation, on Serbian soil, of the origins of the Sarajevo crime. To accept such demands would have meant the end of Serbian independence. Grey described the note as 'the most formidable document I have ever seen addressed by one State to another which is independent'.[122] He was now faced with the danger of Russian intervention on the side of Serbia, and, given the harshness of the Austrian note and the short time-limit—forty-eight hours—given for Serbia's reply, he did not believe that Russia would welcome, still less accept, British advice that she should exercise patience and restraint. While the Germans urged this course on Grey, they did nothing to moderate the policy of Austria. On 24 July Jagow formally proposed to Grey that the two countries should co-operate to localize the war. Germany's desire that Austria should be allowed to enforce her demands upon Serbia without outside interference was an impossible one in the face of Russia's determination to resist an Austrian invasion of Serbia. Eyre Crowe had been suspicious all along of the sincerity of Germany's wish to promote a peaceful settlement of the Austro-Serbian dispute. Austria's ultimatum convinced him that the issue had become a clearcut one between the Triple Alliance and the Triple Entente. He pressed on Grey that the only way to deter Germany from aggressive action was for England to align herself on the side of France and Russia:

> Our interests are tied up with those of France and Russia in this struggle, which is not for the possession of Servia but one between Germany, aiming at a political dictatorship in Europe, and the Powers who desire to retain political freedom.[123]

Grey largely discounted the mounting alarm manifested by his permanent officials and, indeed, he did not entirely take them into his confidence during the crisis.[124] While he recognized, by 24 July, that the situation was becoming serious, he still could not accept Foreign Office assumptions about the true nature of German policy and continued to hope that Anglo-German co-operation might become a reality. He believed that war could be averted if Serbia promised to satisfy Austria's legitimate grievances, while, at the same time, he thought that to give France and Russia assurances of British support in the event of war might encourage them to adopt a provocative attitude in their dealings with the Central Powers. In any case such a declaration would destroy the credibility of his efforts to mediate in the dispute.

His decision to adopt a cautious policy was soon justified by the divisions which developed within the Cabinet over the European crisis. Grey informed his colleagues of the Austrian ultimatum on 24 July and of the possibility that it might, as Asquith put it, result in 'a war in which at least four of the great powers may be involved'.[125] For months past the Cabinet had been absorbed with the steadily deteriorating situation in Ulster, and it was now recalled abruptly to the European situation after a long period of relative indifference to foreign policy. Part of the confusion and incoherence which surrounded the Cabinet's deliberations about the crisis could be attributed to the rapidity with which Europe moved towards war after 24 July, and the Ministers' psychological unreadiness for such an outcome.

During the course of the Cabinet meeting of the 24th, Grey outlined a plan he had formulated whereby he should propose to Lichnowsky mediation between Austria and Russia by the four less interested Powers, England, Germany, France and Italy. He made this proposal to the German Ambassador on the following day. On Sunday the 26th, Nicolson, in charge of the Foreign Office in Grey's absence, became so alarmed by the deteriorating situation that he telegraphed a request to the Governments of Italy, Germany and France to authorize their Ambassadors in London to join Grey in a conference to discuss a settlement of the dispute without delay. Pending the result of this conference, Grey urged that Austria, Russia and Serbia should be asked by the other Powers to refrain from active military measures—Austria had already begun to mobilize, while Sazonov was contemplating 'partial' mobilization as a means of restraining Austria from hasty action.

On 27 July Serbia replied in conciliatory terms to the Austrian note. She accepted most of the latter's demands, except the one which called for Austrian participation in an investigation of Serbian complicity in the assassination plot. The Foreign Office declared this reply to be a reasonable one; but any brief hopes Grey's officials may have entertained that it would pave the way for a peaceful settlement of the crisis were swiftly destroyed when, on the same day, Berchtold rejected it as inadequate and announced the imminence of forceful measures against Serbia. An even more serious blow to Grey's hopes came when, at the same time, Jagow turned down his proposal for four-Power mediation. As far as Germany and Austria were concerned developments were proceeding according to plan, but the British were greatly shaken by these cumulative setbacks to their policy. As Herbert Samuel commented on the 26th, Europe was 'on the brink of the greatest war for a hundred years and possibly the bloodiest war in history'.[126]

Grey informed the Cabinet about these developments on 29 July. Already on the 27th the possibility of a German invasion of France through Belgium had been mooted, for Asquith then noted that the question of Belgian neutrality would be discussed at the next Cabinet meeting. A German violation of Belgium would cut across one of England's few treaty obligations in Europe, and provide her with a clear pretext for intervention in a continental war. The subject thus occupied an important place in the Cabinet's discussions during the last days of peace. The Foreign Office, which had considered Britain's position *vis à vis* Belgian neutrality from time to time before 1914, had adhered to Salisbury's dictum, expressed in 1902, that 'our Treaty obligations will follow our national inclinations—and will not precede them.'[127] The Cabinet reached a similar verdict on the morning of the 29th, when it decided that the question of Belgian neutrality would be 'rather one of policy than of legal obligations'.[128]

The main difficulty was that the Cabinet could not reach agreement on a coherent policy about either Belgium or England's attitude should war break out in Europe. At least half of the Ministers were opposed to British intervention in a continental struggle—they included Lloyd George, Morley, Beauchamp, Simon, Harcourt, Pease, Samuel, McKinnon Wood and John Burns.[129] Thus on 27 July Lloyd George informed Scott that 'there could be no question of our taking part in any war in the first instance'.[130] Asquith and Grey perceived that the Chancellor of the Exchequer was the key to the Cabinet situation: they believed that if he became converted to a policy of intervention, most of the other Ministers would follow his example. Both men realized that to force the issue prematurely would result in the break-up of the Government.

Grey never at any time wavered from his conviction that if Germany attacked France, whether through Belgium or not, England's vital interests dictated that she should come to the assistance of France. Later he threatened to resign if the Cabinet rejected British intervention. He realized on 29 July, however, that such dramatic gestures were as yet unnecessary and self-defeating. Both the Foreign Secretary and Asquith could only hope that developments in Europe during the next few days would somehow determine the issue for the Cabinet. Time was of the essence. The longer war could be averted, the better would be the chance for successful mediation. If, however, mediation failed, the greater would be the possibility that the Cabinet would become converted to intervention. As Masterman appealed to Lloyd George during these anxious days:

> If I *had* to decide now, I would guarantee Belgium and the Fleet Policy. If Germany accepts that, no war. But I am with McKenna and Runciman in fighting for *time*, sooner than break up the Cabinet. 12 hours might find us united. Our collapse would be unthinkable—what is to happen to the Empire if we break to pieces! Do *fight* for unity.[131]

At least Grey could console himself that the Cabinet, on 29 July, did not reject British intervention outright, for it resolved that Britain must keep a free hand to decide whether or not she would act if war broke out. It also authorized precautionary defensive measures to be taken.

There was a short-lived revival of British optimism that a negotiated settlement might still be effected when Jagow insisted that, while he objected to Grey's conference proposal, he still wished to work with England to maintain peace. Bethmann summoned Goschen on the evening of 28 July and informed the Ambassador that he was doing his utmost to promote, both at Vienna and St Petersburg, direct Austro-Russian negotiations, a course which Grey supported. Indeed the Germans were now experiencing a temporary change of heart. They had belatedly come to the conclusion that after all England might intervene on the side of France and Russia, and Grey's warning to Lichnowsky on 29 July that Germany should not gamble on British neutrality confirmed their worst fears. On 29 July the German Foreign Office made frantic efforts to persuade the reluctant Berchtold to enter into direct communication with Russia. But Germany's conversion to a more responsible policy was but a passing phase. By the 30th Bethmann realized that an Austrian retreat at this late stage was impossible and that Germany also could hardly draw back. During the remaining days of peace Bethmann made a few desperate and unavailing efforts to persuade England to remain neutral, and concentrated, at the same time, on trying to saddle France and Britain with the responsibility for a war that was now bound to ensue.[132]

This was partially the explanation for Bethmann's astonishing appeal to Grey, late on 29th July, for British neutrality in the event of a conflagration in return for a German pledge not to secure territorial acquisitions at the expense of France if Germany were victorious. Nevertheless, although Grey replied that such a proposal 'could not for a moment be entertained', he made a final bid to secure Anglo-German co-operation for peaceful purposes —an effort that followed logically from his assumption of the early summer about Germany's increasing vulnerability in the face of a resurgent Russia:

> And if the peace of Europe can be preserved, and this crisis be safely passed, my own endeavour would be to promote some arrangement to which Germany could be a party, by which she could be assured that no hostile or aggressive policy would be pursued against her or her allies by France, Russia, and ourselves, jointly or separately.[133]

Germany ignored the olive branch Grey held out to her. Austria had already declared war on Serbia on 28 July. Now both Russia and Austria were mobilizing against each other, and a fervent debate was raging at St Petersburg as to whether Russia should now mobilize her entire forces. Russian mobilization would be decisive as far as Germany's war plans were concerned. Under the Schlieffen plan France was to be knocked out swiftly before Russia had time to complete her military preparations. Thus for Germany, Russian mobilization meant war, an outcome which Grey seems not to have appreciated. He continued to snatch at every straw to preserve peace, oblivious of the fact that on the continent crucial decisions were rapidly passing from the control of the politicians and civilians to the generals.[134]

As far as Grey's officials were concerned his efforts were thought useless and dangerous. He was deluged with appeals from Nicolson and Crowe for England to range herself immediately alongside France and Russia. Grey recognized, however, that it would be difficult to persuade British public opinion that the country should intervene in a war resulting from a Russo-Austrian dispute over Serbia, a country in which Britain had little interest. He warned Cambon on 29 July that even if France became embroiled in a war with Germany on account of her treaty obligations to Russia, England was in no way committed to interfere on the side of France.

On 31 July when it became clear that Austro-Russian negotiations were unlikely to take place, he reverted to his earlier plan for mediation by the four less interested Powers, this time to secure for Austria the fullest satisfaction of her demands on Serbia. Meanwhile he hoped that even if Austria occupied Belgrade, she would make no effort to advance further into the country and that all the Powers would suspend further military operations. When, during the evening of the 31st, the German Emperor offered to restrain Austria if England would persuade Russia to delay full mobilization, Grey, Asquith and Churchill woke the King at 1.30 a.m. on 1 August, and persuaded him to appeal direct to the Russian Emperor. The appeal was made too late, for Nicholas II had already, on the 30th, signed the order for general mobilization on the 31st, and he would not reverse the process.[135]

The Cabinet met on the morning of Saturday 1 August to consider British policy in the light of this confused situation. The majority of the Ministers remained opposed to British involvement should war ensue. Only Grey, Haldane, Churchill and Asquith supported British intervention irrespective of what happened to Belgium. Nevertheless, as Asquith put it, 'the main controversy pivots upon Belgium and its neutrality'.[136] The difficulty was that not until 1 August was the Cabinet certain that Belgium would either defend her neutrality or call upon the Treaty powers to assist her in her defence.[137] Even as late as the 2nd the Belgians were claiming that they doubted that Germany would attack them.[138]

On 31 July, Grey enquired of France and Germany whether each was prepared to respect Belgian neutrality in the event of war. While France promised that she would do so, Germany refused to give any statement as to her attitude towards that country if hostilities broke out. Jagow again rejected Grey's appeal for four-Power mediation, on the ground that the entire situation had since been altered by Russia's mobilization. On the 31st Germany warned Russia that unless she stopped her mobilization within 12 hours, Germany would be forced to mobilize. On the following day Germany declared war on Russia.

The Cabinet met again on the Sunday morning. According to Samuel, Grey was so 'outraged' at these demonstrations of Germany's aggressive policy that he at last called upon the Ministers to agree that England should support France and Russia.[139] Here at least was an issue on which the Cabinet non-interventionists and the waverers could come together. Harcourt appealed to Lloyd George, '*You must now speak for us.* Grey wants us to go to war *without any violation of Belgium*.'[140] Nevertheless, despite the Ministers' continued opposition to British participation in the European war, Herbert Samuel was able to persuade the Cabinet to agree to Grey's minimum demand that the British navy should defend France's northern coasts from a German naval attack— Cambon had raised the question on the previous day. Some Ministers intended that this should be the utmost that England would do to assist France, and it at least satisfied the guilty consciences of those politicians who believed that England had blundered into some kind of moral commitment to France as a result of the fleet transfers. It was too much, however, for John Burns, who resigned, although he was prevailed upon to remain in the Government until the evening.

The British pledge to France about her northern coasts did not commit England to war, and Germany was even prepared to agree to it. Samuel, however, hit upon a scheme which he hoped (or pretended) would enable England to escape involvement and, at the same time, render more tangible assistance to France. He discussed his plan with Lloyd George, Harcourt, Beauchamp, Simon, McKinnon Wood, Pease and Morley at lunch after the Sunday morning Cabinet meeting. Samuel believed that if England followed up her guarantee of the northern coast of France by announcing that she would go to war with any power violating Belgian neutrality, this would deter Germany from attacking France through Belgium, and force her to concentrate her troops on the narrow and more easily defensible Franco-

German frontier. France would thereby, he thought, be rendered 'the greatest of all services', and at the same time Britain's vital interests would be safeguarded. He wrote: 'if we can achieve this, without firing a shot, we shall have accomplished a brilliant stroke of policy. . . If we fail it will be Germany's fault—my conscience will be easy.'[141] It was accepted by Lloyd George, who later argued that in these circumstances France would have found it easy to defend her frontier against Germany, and that as a result deadlock would have ensued on the western front. England could then have come forward to insist that Germany and France make peace.[142] Morley was totally opposed to the scheme, which he saw would make British involvement more rather than less likely. He feared that a Triple Entente victory would end in Russia's domination of Europe. Samuel remarked that Morley 'is now so old that the views he expresses are sadly inconsequent and inconsistent'.[143]

The Cabinet met in the evening of the 2nd from 6.30 to 8.30 and resolved, in accordance with Samuel's plan, that any substantial violation of Belgian neutrality would compel England to intervene. Evidently Lloyd George thought that minor frontier violations of Belgian territory might be overlooked.[144] Samuel's manoeuvre failed. On the Monday morning the Cabinet learnt that Germany had delivered an ultimatum at Brussels the previous evening, demanding that the Belgians permit the passage of her troops, and that the Belgians had announced their intention of defending their country. Germany's fatal move united the bulk of the Cabinet behind Asquith and Grey. While Morley, Beauchamp and Simon had already decided to join Burns in resignation, Lloyd George was at last converted to intervention on the side of Belgium. While he subsequently wrote that Belgium was the sole issue which had made up his mind, no doubt strategic considerations played a large part in his decision, in the same way as they had done during the Agadir crisis.[145] The majority of the Ministers followed the Chancellor into the interventionist camp. The Asquith–Grey policy of patient waiting had finally triumphed.

Events now moved swiftly. The Cabinet spent the morning of the 3rd in drawing up the details of Grey's somewhat long-winded speech on the subject of British policy towards the war, and towards Belgium, which he delivered to a packed House of Commons in the afternoon. Later came the news that Germany had declared war on France and that the King of the Belgians had appealed to King George for 'diplomatic intervention' on behalf of Belgium. This was supplied by the rather mildly phrased British note to Germany of 4 August, which required Germany to withdraw her demands on Belgium and to respect Belgian neutrality. A reply was requested by midnight (11.00 p.m. G.M.T.). The British 'ultimatum' was ignored by Germany, who announced her intention of invading Belgium. Simon and Beauchamp had already withdrawn their resignations. Scott met Simon after the Cabinet meeting of the 3rd:

> He began at once by saying that he had been entirely deceived about Germany, and that I ought to know that the evidence was over-whelming that the party which had got control of the direction of affairs throughout the crisis had deliberately played for and pro-voked war... [Lloyd George] confirmed all that Simon had said about the provocative attitude of German diplomacy . . . the violation of Belgian territory had completely altered the situation.[146]

The British ultimatum expired at 11.00 on 4 August without any reply from Germany, beyond news from Brussels that the German army had advanced across the Belgian frontier. England was at war.

Conclusion

Grey's policy during July and early August 1914 has received considerable attention from his critics. On the one extreme, there were subsequent accusations of Morley and Loreburn that the secret ties he had made with France in the previous years saddled England with a moral obligation to go to her assistance in an unjust war. On the other, there were the complaints of Lloyd George that Grey's weak handling of the situation before 4 August, and his failure to warn Germany earlier that England would go to war over Belgium, made it more certain that Germany would gamble on war.[147] This charge was later taken up by Albertini, who maintained that England left it too late to warn Germany about Belgium, and that an earlier declaration on the subject might have stayed Germany's hand.[148]

The Morley–Loreburn accusations have already been dealt with. Grey had made it clear to France that England was in no way obligated to her, and even if there had existed a degree of moral commitment resulting from the naval convention of 1913 this was surely extinguished by the Cabinet's agreement about France's northern coasts. As for the Anglo-French military conversations, these did not commit England to go to war on the side of France. The statements of Lloyd George and Albertini have no validity in view of the fact that before 2 August the Cabinet could not make up its mind about Belgium, or indeed anything else. There was also a large area of doubt as to how Belgium would react to a violation of her neutrality. Harcourt was reported to have stated on Sunday 2 August that if Belgium did not resist a German invasion, England could not be 'more Belgian than the Belgians, and rescue them if they did not want to be rescued'.[149] Grey wanted to be accepted as a mediator in the dispute: British declarations and threats would not have conduced to the success of his efforts.

In any case mediation was, as he discovered too late, out of the question in view of Germany's attitude. The Germans misled him throughout: in failing to restrain Austria while pretending to do so, and in assuring him that they were willing to co-operate with England to maintain peace. By 29 July Bethmann realized that he had miscalculated about England's neutrality, but he had in fact received sufficient warnings in the past from Grey that England might not be able to remain aloof from continental war, warnings which he chose to ignore in 1914. By 29 July Germany's military preparations were well under way, and the German General Staff was not much concerned with the possibility of British military assistance to France. Moltke believed that the British army was a negligible quantity, and that the German army would be able to wipe out the French before British naval strength could be applied effectively.[150]

At least, as Professor Medlicott has pointed out, there could be no complaint that Grey had attempted to move ahead of either public opinion, or the Cabinet, in July 1914, or to force the issue in any way: indeed he 'waited scrupulously for the cabinet to lead him'.[151] By 2 August public opinion was moving in favour of British intervention: by the 3rd the Cabinet had come round. The strain of waiting for a decision was considerable for Grey. C. F. G. Masterman related that at one Cabinet meeting during the crisis, Grey had burst into tears—'an extraordinary thing in a man so reserved'.[152]

There was good reason for Grey's emotional reaction to the events of July 1914. Grey was a man of peace—not even his worst enemies ever accused him of being a warmonger. His foreign policy had been dedicated to avoiding involvement in war in Europe: before 1912 by alignment with France and Russia, after 1912 by attempting to reassure Germany that her fears of Triple Entente hostility were unreal. In July 1914 he realized that he had failed. His patient policy kept the Liberals united in July; but the events of 1914-18 destroyed their cohesion altogether, as the fundamental principles of Liberalism proved incompatible with the waging of total war.

Notes

CHAPTER 1

1. G. W. Monger, *The End of Isolation* (London, 1963) pp. 77–81.
2. See C. J. Lowe, *The Reluctant Imperialists* (London, 1967) I, p. 8.
3. See D. Judd, *Balfour and the British Empire* (London, 1968) p. 35, 'the most pressing and obvious need was that of reform at home.' A. J. Balfour succeeded Salisbury as Prime Minister in July 1902. He set up the Committee of Imperial Defence on 18 December to survey and co-ordinate the military needs of the British Empire. A year later he became its chairman and in 1904 it was provided with a secretariat. F. A. Johnson, *Defence by Committee, The British Committee of Imperial Defence, 1885–1959* (London, 1960) pp. 53–65.
4. At least until the Board discovered that Japan was retarding her naval construction programme.
5. I. A. Nish, *The Anglo-Japanese Alliance* (London, 1966) pp. 256–7; Monger, pp. 71–2.
6. For details of the Anglo-Russian rivalry in Persia and Central Asia see Chapter 3, pp. 56–76.
7. 'By the autumn of 1902, therefore, public opinion, the government, and the Admiralty, were as one in viewing the German fleet as a potential menace far greater than the fleets of the Dual Alliance.' A. J. Marder, *The Anatomy of British Sea Power* (London, 1964 ed.) p. 465.
8. Lord Newton, *Lord Lansdowne* (London, 1929) pp. 247–8.
9. See p. 101.
10. Newton, p. 260.
11. With rare unanimity a joint Admiralty, War Office, India Office, and Foreign Office conference on 19 November agreed that the line should be supported as 'the most effective check to Russian progress towards South Persia'. Quoted in Monger, p. 119.
12. Newton, pp. 243, 249–54; Monger, pp. 122–3; Maybelle Kennedy Chapman, *Great Britain and the Bagdad Railway, 1888–1914* (Northampton, Mass., 1948) pp. 20–70.
13. Christopher Andrew, *Théophile Delcassé and the Making of the Entente Cordiale* (London, 1968) pp. 194–5.
14. Julian Amery, *The Life of Joseph Chamberlain*, IV, 1901–3 (London, 1931) pp. 171–86; Vols V and VI, *Joseph Chamberlain and the Tariff Reform Campaign* (London, 1969) pp. 137, 184–92, 326.
15. See M. S. Anderson, *The Eastern Question* (London, 1966) pp. 270–2.
16. See Chapter 3, pp. 77–81.
17. In February Balfour finally abandoned the doctrine of the defence of Constantinople; it was 'not one of the primary naval or military interests of this country'. Monger, p. 117.
18. Sir Sidney Lee, *King Edward VII* (London, 1927) II, p. 282; Nish, pp. 275–6;

Monger, pp. 147–52. The Army Council, however, recommended that Britain range herself alongside Japan.

19. Monger, pp. 147–55; Nish, pp. 273–82.
20. Balfour to Spencer Wilkinson, 3 January 1904, Balfour MSS., no. 49747.
21. Mallet to Balfour, 24 February 1904, Balfour MSS., no. 49747.
22. Lansdowne to Balfour, 24 December 1903, Balfour MSS., no. 49728.
23. Monger, p. 152.
24. *Ibid.*, p. 153.
25. Cromer to Balfour, 15 October 1903, Balfour MSS., no. 49747.
26. Monger, pp. 157–9; Newton, pp. 283–92; Andrew, pp. 212–13. For further details see Samuel R. Williamson, Jr., *The Politics of Grand Strategy: Britain and France Prepare for War, 1904–1914* (Cambridge, Mass., 1969) pp. 1–15.
27. The phrase was Lansdowne's; 27 July 1904, Newton, p. 313. Doc. 1.
28. For a detailed account see John A. White, *The Diplomacy of the Russo-Japanese War* (Princeton, 1965).
29. The Prime Minister wrote to Lansdowne in January 1905, 'I am, on broad moral grounds, very anxious to do all we can to put an end to the war. But I have to admit that, from a narrowly national point of view, the balance of advantage I suspect, is on the side of continued hostilities.' Balfour to Lansdowne, 24 January 1905, Balfour MSS., no. 49729. Doc. 2.
30. Quoted in Monger, p. 161.
31. Text of the 'second alliance' in Nish, pp. 331–3. Doc. 3.
32. Quoted in Newton, p. 338. Balfour believed that the ill-feeling on the British side stemmed from German press attacks on British policy, Germany's naval competition, and her restless diplomacy. 'Those who entertain such views cannot but regard with suspicion every movement of German diplomacy. For they conceive that its end is to stir up strife between us and other Powers, in the hope that Germany may profit by the exhaustion consequent on a conflict which she has occasioned but not shared.' Balfour to Lascelles, end January 1905, Balfour MSS., no. 49747.
33. For a detailed account on the ensuing complications, see Eugene W. Anderson, *The First Moroccan Crisis, 1904–6* (Chicago, 1930). Doc. 4.
34. Andrew, pp. 256–73.
35. Mallet urged Balfour that 'the peace of Europe and our security depend entirely on the attitude we observe and on our loyalty to the understanding with France.' Mallet to Balfour, 6 May 1905, Balfour MSS., no. 49747.
36. Quoted in Monger, p. 197.
37. Andrew, pp. 281–8; Williamson, pp. 37–40.
38. Lee, II, p. 344. Doc. 5.
39. Monger, pp. 186–235. Doc. 6.
40. Ronald Hyam, *Elgin and Churchill at the Colonial Office, 1905–1908. The Watershed of the Empire Commonwealth* (London, 1968) pp. 49–51.
41. See G. M. Trevelyan, *Grey of Fallodon* (London, 1937) for a sympathetic biography, and Grey's own memoirs, *Twenty-Five Years, 1892–1916*, 2 vols (London, 1926).
42. David Lloyd George, *War Memoirs*, 2 vols (London, 1936) I, pp. 28, 60; G. P. Gooch, *Before the War* (London, 1936–38) II, p. 109; Lord Loreburn, *How the War Came* (London, 1936) pp. 19–20; John Morley, *Memorandum on Resignation* (London, 1928) pp. 17–18.
43. Grey noted in 1908 that neither Salisbury nor Rosebery went abroad much. He admitted, however, in 1925 that 'I hated all ceremonial so much that I persuaded myself that it was not a bounden duty for me to go.' Grey to Spender 2 June 1925, Spender MSS., no. 246388.

44. J. L. Hammond, *C. P. Scott of the Manchester Guardian* (London, 1936) p. 151.
45. Grey to Lowther, Constantinople, 12 September 1908, F.O. 800/79.
46. For a recent account see S. J. S. Cookey, *Britain and the Congo Question, 1885–1914* (London, 1968).
47. The work eventually cost him his eyesight.
48. Grey, I, p. 133.
49. Grey to Rodd, Rome, desp. 5, 16 January 1911, F.O. 371/792.
50. On this subject see Zara Steiner, *The Foreign Office and Foreign Policy, 1898–1914* (Cambridge, 1969). There is also much material in Monger.
51. Steiner, pp. 70–82.
52. On Anglo-German relations see B.D. III, Appendix A. Also Monger, pp. 313–15; and Steiner, pp. 68–9, for Sanderson's riposte.
53. He wrote to J. A. Spender in October 1905 that 'I think we are running a real risk of losing France and not gaining Germany who won't want us if she can detach France from us.' Grey to Spender 19 October 1905, Spender MSS., no. 46389. Doc. 7.
54. See S. L. Mayer, 'Anglo-German Rivalry at the Algeçiras Conference', in *Britain and Germany in Africa, Imperial Rivalry and Colonial Rule*, ed. by P. Gifford and Wm. Roger Louis (New Haven, 1967).
55. Trevelyan, p. 138.
56. Haldane, as Secretary for War, was, of course, even more closely involved in the talks than Grey.
57. Lowe, I, pp. 16–17; Monger, pp. 236–56; Grey, I, Chapter 6; Williamson, pp. 59–88. 'The Cabinet was concerned with more pressing issues and was deliberately not organized to keep a tight control over its members.' Doreen Collins, *Aspects of British Politics, 1904–1919* (Oxford, 1965) p. 130.
58. Grey to Nicolson, 21 December 1905, in Harold Nicolson, *Lord Carnock* (London, 1930) p. 175.
59. The three were Austria, Germany and Morocco.
60. Nicolson, *Lord Carnock*, p. 191.
61. Monger, p. 278.
62. Grey, I, p. 111.
63. Mayer, pp. 236–41.
64. Trevelyan, pp. 114–15.
65. Bertie to Nicolson, 15 March 1911, F.O. 800/186.
66. Grey, I, p. 113.
67. Monger, pp. 328–9.
68. Gorst to Cromer, 6 June 1908, Cromer MSS., F.O. 633/14.
69. An indifference shared by most of his colleagues after 1906, Hyam, pp. 515 and 529.
70. At the same time British traders often had a poor reputation abroad. Sir Gerard Lowther, Ambassador at Constantinople after 1908, frequently complained of the poor calibre of British sales representatives in Turkey, the lethargy of British exporters, and their unwillingness to tailor their products to suit local needs, in contrast, for instance, to Italian producers.
71. Minute by Crowe on Sir Reginald Lister, Tangier, to Grey, desp. 113, 13 May 1908, F.O. 371/696. Grey merely followed traditional British policy in eschewing official interference in the affairs of other countries on behalf of British traders, financiers etc. except to ensure fair and equal treatment for British interests. There were of course exceptions, such as in politically sensitive areas like Morocco, Persia, Turkey and China, where the Government might sometimes urge financiers to invest in loans. But this pressure often failed in its intent, for, as Hardinge and Grey realized, British capitalists preferred to risk

their money in North and South America. For a full discussion of this question
see D. C. M. Platt, *Finance, Trade and Politics in British Foreign Policy, 1815–1914*
(Oxford, 1968).

72. Grey, I, pp. 117–18.
73. Grey to Crewe, 17 June 1908, F.O. 800/91.
74. Minute by Grey on Rodd, Rome to Grey, desp. 47, 10 February 1909, F.O. 371/599.
75. Lowe, I, p. 8.

CHAPTER 2

1. Monger, p. 267.
2. Grey to Bertie, desp. 402, 26 August 1908, G. P. Gooch and H. Temperley, [B]ritish [D]ocuments on the Origins of the First World War, 1898–1914, 11 vols (1929–38) VI, no. 120. (All references refer to numbers of documents cited, unless otherwise stated.)
3. Minute by Grey on Goschen to Hardinge, 13 May 1910, Hardinge MSS. (1910).
4. Arthur J. Marder, *From the Dreadnought to Scapa Flow* (London, 1961–9) I, pp. 43–5, 56–7.
5. Grey to Knollys, 12 November 1906, Royal Archives, V.I.C. W 50/45. Doc. 8.
6. Marder, *From the Dreadnought*, I, pp. 130–1; E. L. Woodward, *Great Britain and the German Navy* (London, 1934) p. 155. These two books contain much useful information on Anglo-German naval and political relations down to 1914, as does Monger to 1908.
7. Crowe to Dilke, 15 October 1907, Dilke MSS., no. 43919.
8. Reay to Campbell-Bannerman, 22 October 1907, Campbell-Bannerman MSS., no. 41242.
9. For a recent evaluation of Haldane see Stephen E. Koss, *Lord Haldane, Scapegoat for Liberalism* (London, 1969). Doc. 9.
10. Morley to Minto, 8 January 1908, Morley MSS., EUR.D. 573/3.
11. Monger, pp. 325–31; D. A. Hamer, *John Morley. Liberal Intellectual in Politics* (Oxford, 1968) pp. 345–6.
12. Grey to Asquith, 5 February 1909, Asquith MSS., vol. I.
13. Minute by Crowe on Lascelles to Grey, desp. 9, 9 January 1908, F.O. 371/457.
14. Hardinge to Lascelles, 19 May 1908, Hardinge MSS. (1908).
15. For details of Lloyd George's influence on foreign policy in these years see M. L. Dockrill, 'David Lloyd George and Foreign Policy before 1914', in *Lloyd George: Twelve Essays* (ed.) A. J. P. Taylor (London, 1971).
16. Grey to Asquith, 22 August 1908, F.O. 800/100. Doc. 10.
17. Grey to Asquith, 26 August 1908, F.O. 800/100.
18. Grey to Bertie, 12 November 1908, B.D. VI, 135.
19. Marder, *From the Dreadnought*, I, pp. 151–6. The reports of German acceleration were in fact greatly exaggerated. The four contingent battleships were authorized in July.
20. Grey to Churchill, 22 April 1909, F.O. 800/89.
21. Minute by Grey on Goschen to Grey, desp. 141, 16 April 1909, B.D. VI, 174. Doc. 11.
22. Hardinge to Goschen, Berlin, 3 May 1909, Hardinge MSS. (1909).
23. Grey to Goschen, 5 May 1910, B.D. VI, 361. Doc. 12.
24. Nicolson to Goschen, 27 October 1910, F.O. 800/344.
25. Asquith to the King, 9 March 1911, Cabinet MSS., Cab. 41/33/5. Docs 13, 14.

26. See E. W. Edwards, 'The Franco-German Agreement on Morocco, 1909', *English Historical Review*, vol. LXXVIII, July 1963, pp. 483–513.
27. Hardinge to Lister, Tangier, 21 January 1909, Hardinge MSS. (1909).
28. Monger, pp. 321–2.
29. Minute by Langley on Spanish Ambassador to Grey, 2 March 1910, F.O. 371/930.
30. Minute by Crowe on Colonial Office to Foreign Office, 7 January 1911, F.O. 371–1116.
31. Hyam, pp. 202–3. The question was eventually settled in 1913. France agreed to give up her rights to trade arms in Muscat, England to compensate French arms traders for their losses. For details see Briton Cooper Busch, *Britain and the Persian Gulf, 1894–1914* (Berkeley, 1967) pp. 270–303.
32. Minute by Grey on Bertie to Grey, desp. 187, 19 April 1912, F.O. 371/1365.
33. Crewe to Hardinge, 5 October 1911, Hardinge MSS. (1911).
34. Minute by Hardinge on L. O. Carnegie, Paris to Grey, desp. 258, 1 July 1910, F.O. 371/896. Similar complaints were voiced by Salisbury about Germany's colonial demands in 1898, Lowe, I, p. 219.
35. Minute by Grey on Captain Mark Kerr, R.N., to Grey, 30 March 1911, F.O. 800/108.
36. France was kept informed of the progress, or lack of progress, of the Anglo-German negotiations. Grey also persuaded Churchill, whose pro-German views were distrusted in France, against visiting Paris in 1909. A year earlier he had even rejected a Portuguese request to send a British representative to attend the 1909 celebrations in commemoration of Anglo-Portuguese victories during the peninsular war, lest the French should be offended.
37. For a full account of the crisis provoked by this action see I. C. Barlow, *The Agadir Crisis* (North Carolina, 1940). For the German side see Joanne Stafford Mortimer, 'Commercial Interests and German Diplomacy in the Agadir Crisis', *Historical Journal*, X, 4 (1967) pp. 440–56. Williamson, pp. 143–66.
38. Minute by Crowe on Bunsen, Madrid to Grey, tel. 8, 7 April 1911, F.O. 371/1154. Doc. 15.
39. Grey to de Salis, Berlin, tel. 127, 4 July 1911, B.D. VII, 347.
40. Eric Drummond to Hardinge, 13 July 1911, Hardinge MSS. (1911).
41. Asquith to Grey, 18 July 1911, F.O. 800/100.
42. Minute by Crowe, on Bertie to Grey, tel. 103, 18 July 1911, B.D. VII, 392.
43. Asquith to the King, 19 July 1911, Cabinet Papers, Cab. 41/33/22. Doc. 16.
44. Crowe to Bertie, 20 July 1911, F.O. 800/160. Doc. 17.
45. Grey to Asquith, 19 July 1911, B.D. VII, 399.
46. Grey to Bertie, draft of tel. 183, 20 July 1911, F.O. 800/52. Grey subsequently deleted this sentence before despatching the telegram.
47. Asquith to the King, 21 July 1911, Asquith MSS., vol. 6.
48. Relevant portion of speech in *Great Lives Observed; Lloyd George*, ed. Martin Gilbert (London, 1968) p. 46.
49. Cf. A. J. P. Taylor, *The Struggle for Mastery in Europe, 1848–1918* (Oxford, 1954) p. 471. Lloyd George stated at the time and later that his warning was directed to Germany. *The War Memoirs of David Lloyd George*, I, pp. 43–5; Lord Riddell, *More Pages from My Diary, 1908–14* (London, 1934) pp. 20–1.
50. Grey to McKenna, 24 July 1911, B.D. VII, 637.
51. Churchill to Lloyd George, 31 August 1911, quoted in Randolph S. Churchill, *Winston S. Churchill*, II, *Young Statesmen, 1901–1914* (London, 1967) pp. 530–1. Docs 18, 19.
52. Committee of Imperial Defence, Minutes of 114th Meeting, 23 August 1911, C.I.D. Papers, Cab 38/19/49. Docs 26, 27, 28.
53. McKenna took Churchill's place at the Home Office.

54. Sir C. E. Callwell, *Field Marshal Sir Henry Wilson, His Life and Diaries* (London, 1927) I, Chapter VI, pp. 86–108. For a recent account of these developments see Williamson, Chapter 7.

55. Report of the sub-committee . . . on the Military needs of the Empire, 24 July 1909, C.I.D. papers, Cab. 33/15/15.

56. War Office to Foreign Office, 26 November 1910, F.O. 371/990.

57. Nicolson to Grey, 12 September 1911, F.O. 800/93; Nicolson to Hardinge, 14 September 1911, F.O. 800/350. Docs. 20, 21, 22, 23, 24.

58. Marder, *From the Dreadnought*, I, pp. 250–1.

59. Diary of John Burns, 2 November 1911, Burns MSS., no. 46333. Doc. 29.

60. Churchill to Grey, 4 November 1911, F.O. 800/87.

61. Grey to Asquith, 13 September 1911, Asquith MSS., vol. 13. Doc. 25.

62. Grey to Bertie, 8 November 1911, B.D. VII, 631.

63. Churchill to Cassel, 7 January 1912, B.D. VI, 492. See R. T. B. Langhorne, 'The Naval Question in Anglo-German Relations, 1912–1914', *Historical Journal* (1970). Doc. 31.

64. For a recent discussion see Koss, pp. 65–94.

65. Grey to Churchill, 29 January 1912, Lloyd George Papers, C/3/15/14.

66. Asquith to the King, 3 February 1912, Cabinet Papers, Cab. 41/33/34. Doc. 32.

67. Diary of Lord Haldane's visit to Berlin, 10 February 1912, B.D. VI, p. 506.

68. Minute by Crowe on Captain Watson, to Goschen, 8 February 1912, F.O., 371/1372. Doc. 33.

69. Memorandum by Bertie, 16 February 1912, F.O. 800/171. Docs 34, 35.

70. Paper by Winston Churchill, 17 February 1912, Lloyd George Papers, C/3/15/15.

71. Asquith to the King, 21 February 1912, Cabinet Papers, Cab. 41/33/37.

72. Memorandum by Harcourt, 9 March 1912, Harcourt MSS., Box 14.

73. 'Interview with Haldane and Grey, 11 p.m.–12.15 a.m.' 14 March 1912, Harcourt MSS., Box 14.

74. Grey again refused to agree to a neutrality clause, although he told the Cabinet that he was prepared to inform Metternich that 'so long as Bethmann Hollweg is Chancellor we will cooperate with Germany for the peace of Europe', a pledge he tried to keep. Asquith to the King, 16 March 1912, Cabinet papers, Cab. 41/33/41; 'Rough Notes of Cabinet Meeting', 16 March 1912, Harcourt MSS., Box 14. McKenna and Loreburn supported Harcourt's efforts to secure an 'extension of formula', *ibid.*

75. Asquith to the King, 30 March 1912, Cabinet Papers, Cab. 41/33/45.

76. Although Asquith wrote to Grey on 10 April that further negotiations seemed pointless since, 'nothing, I believe, will meet her purpose which falls short of a promise on our part of neutrality; a promise we cannot give. And she makes no firm or solid offer, even in exchange for that.' Asquith to Grey, 10 April 1912, B.D. VI, 571.

77. Nicolson to Goschen, 1 April 1912, B.D. VI, 562.

78. Nicolson to Goschen, 16 April 1912, F.O. 800/355.

79. Lowe, I, pp. 219–24.

80. On this question see Roger Louis, 'Great Britain and German expansion in Africa, 1884–1919', pp. 36–8, and Jacques Willequet, 'Anglo-German Rivalry and Portuguese Africa', pp. 259–73, in *Britain and Germany in Africa*. No mention is made in these essays of Harcourt's part in the transactions of 1912 and 1913.

81. Nicolson to Bertie, 6 April 1912, F.O. 800/171. Doc. 36.

82. Memorandum by Churchill, 'The Mediterranean Fleet', 15 March 1911, Cabinet Papers, Cab. 37/105/27. Doc. 37.

83. 'Memorandum on the naval situation by Reginald McKenna', 24 June 1912, Cabinet Papers, Cab. 37/111/79. Doc. 38.
84. 'Memorandum on the naval situation, III, by Churchill', 25 June 1912, Cabinet Papers, Cab. 37/111/80; Memorandum by Reginald McKenna, 3 July 1912, Cabinet Papers, Cab. 37/111/86.
85. See Chapter 3, pp. 92–5.
86. Churchill to Haldane, 3 and 6 May 1912, Haldane MSS., no. 5900.
87. Kitchener to Grey, 2 June 1912, B.D.X. II, 392.
88. J. E. B. Seely replaced Haldane as Secretary of War during the summer on the latter's appointment to the Lord Chancellorship.
89. Report of the Committee of Imperial Defence, 117th meeting, 4 July 1912, C.I.D. papers, Cab. 38/21/26.
90. Churchill was forced to introduce a supplementary naval estimate for an extra £5m. in July 1912 to meet the additional strain imposed by the German *novelle*.
91. Asquith to the King, 5, 12, 16 (and annexe) July 1912, Cabinet Papers, Cab. 41/33/56–59. Doc. 39.
92. Memorandum by Bertie, 25 and 27 July 1912, F.O. 800/165. Doc. 40.
93. Asquith to Grey, 11 October 1912, B.D.X. II, 412.
94. Asquith to the King, 1 November 1912, Cab. 41/33/66.
95. Asquith to the King, 20 and 21 November, Cab. 41/33/71, Grey to Cambon, 22 November 1912, Cambon to Grey, 23 November 1912, B.D.X. II, 416–17. See also Williamson, Chapters 11 and 12, for a detailed account of these developments. He concludes that by 1913 'the Entente Cordiale . . . had progressively evolved into a friendly partnership with military and naval features directed against Germany', p. 299.
96. Nicolson to Goschen, 21 May 1912, F.O. 800/356. Doc. 41.

CHAPTER 3

1. Lowe, I, p. 231.
2. *Ibid.*, Chapter 4.
3. Firuz Kazemzadeh, *Russia and Britain in Persia, 1864–1914: A Study in Imperialism* (New Haven, 1968) pp. 261–326. An interesting account, marred by intemperate and often unjust attacks on Grey's policy. Very weak on the period after 1912.
4. England was also threatened in the Gulf by Turkey's efforts to recover her full sovereignty in the area after 1898, and by the interest shown by the Anatolian Railway Company in Kuweit as a suitable terminus for its line from Constantinople. See Briton Cooper Busch, *Britain and the Persian Gulf, 1894–1914* (Berkeley, 1967) for a full history.
5. Alistair Lamb, *Britain and Chinese Central Asia, The Road to Lhasa 1767 to 1905* (London, 1960) and *The MacMahon Line* (London, 1968) I, pp. 3–8.
6. David Dilks, *Curzon in India* (London, 1969) I, Chapters 5–7.
7. 27 December 1901, quoted in Kazemzadeh, p. 442.
8. See Chapter 1, p. 4.
9. Dilks, II, pp. 62–5.
10. Busch, pp. 118–77, 221–62; Kazemzadeh, p. 443.
11. Platt, pp. 239–40.
12. Derek William Spring, 'Anglo-Russian Relations in Persia, 1909–1915' (unpublished doctoral thesis, London, 1968) pp. 23–9.
13. A. Lamb, *Britain and Chinese Central Asia*, pp. 239–313. See also Parshotam

Mehra, *The Younghusband Mission, An Interpretation* (London, 1968) and Dilks, II, pp. 74–101.

14. Dilks, II, pp. 150–76.
15. Curzon to Brodrick, 2 March 1905, quoted in Dilks, II, p. 171.
16. *Ibid.*, pp. 227–42.
17. Quoted in Monger, p. 285.
18. Minto to Morley, 23 June and 23 September 1908, Morley MSS., EUR. D. 573/16 and 17.
19. Lowe, I, p. 203.
20. For further details see R. P. Churchill, *The Anglo-Russian Convention of 1907* (Iowa, 1939), Beryl J. Williams, 'The Strategic Background to the Anglo-Russian Entente of August 1907', *Historical Journal*, IX, 3 (1966) and Monger, Chapter 11.
21. See Max Beloff, *Lucien Wolf and the Anglo-Russian Entente, 1907–1914* (London, 1951). Doc. 42.
22. Hardinge to Nicolson, 28 October 1908, F.O. 800/341.
23. The following account is based on the Foreign Office Confidential Print for Persia, 1907–14, B.D.X. I and II, Kazemzadeh, Spring, and Nikki R. Keddie, 'British Policy and the Iranian Opposition, 1091–1907', *Journal of Modern History* (no. 39, 1967).
24. Nicolson to Hardinge, 17 August 1911, Hardinge, MSS. (1911). Doc. 43.
25. Grey to O'Beirne, St Petersburg, private tel., 5 July 1909, F.O. 800/73.
26. Grey to O'Beirne, private tel., 13 June 1910, F.O. 800/73.
27. Nicolson to O'Beirne, 9 and 22 November 1910, F.O. 800/344.
28. On 5 September 1911 the ex-Shah's forces were defeated by a Nationalist army, which had been organized by Shuster. This further incensed the Russians against him. Doc. 54.
29. Grey to Hardinge, 28 January 1912, F.O. 800/94.
30. The Shah left Persia in February 1912.
31. Grey to Buchanan, 3 April 1912, F.O. 800/74.
32. Buchanan to Grey, 18 April 1912, F.O. 800/74.
33. Nicolson to Buchanan, 23 April 1912, Nicolson to O'Beirne, 8 May 1912, F.O. 800/355 and 356.
34. Crewe to Hardinge, 5 September 1912, Hardinge MSS. (1912).
35. Lamb, *The McMahon Line*, II, Chapter XXII. Doc. 55.
36. Grey to J. A. Spender, 24 September 1912, F.O. 800/111.
37. Crewe to Hardinge, 26 September 1912, Hardinge, MSS. (1912). Docs 56, 57, 58.
38. Grey to Nicolson, 27 September 1912, F.O. 800/358.
39. Memorandum by C. P. Scott, 1 December 1911, 22 January 1912, Scott MSS. no. 50901.
40. See Lowe, I, pp. 196–203.
41. The following account is taken from Douglas Dakin, *The Greek Struggle in Macedonia 1897–1913* (Thessaloniki, 1967) pp. 46 ff. Doc. 44.
42. Cf. Lowe, I, p. 35.
43. F. R. Bridge, 'The Diplomatic Relations Between Great Britain and Austria-Hungary, 1906–1912' (unpublished Ph.D. thesis, London, 1966) p. 47; A. J. Dorey, 'Radical Liberal Criticism of British Foreign Policy 1906–1914' (unpublished D.Phil. thesis, Oxford, 1964) pp. 83–94.
44. Folke Lindberg, *Scandinavia in Great Power Politics 1905–1908* (Stockholm, 1958) p. 99.
45. Hardinge to Nicolson, 7 January 1908, F.O. 800/341.
46. Minute by Mallet on O'Beirne to Grey, desp. 256, 2 June 1908, F.O. 371/517.

47. See Feroz Ahmad, *The Young Turks: The Committee of Union and Progress in Turkish Politics, 1908–1914* (Oxford, 1969).
48. Grey to Lowther, 11 August 1908, B.D.V., Ed. Add., 207. Doc. 45.
49. For details of the ensuing crisis see B. E. Schmitt, *The Annexation of Bosnia, 1908–1909* (Cambridge, 1937) and M. B. Cooper, 'British Policy in the Balkans', *Historical Journal*, VII, p. 2 (1964).
50. Grey to Asquith, 5 October 1908, F.O. 800/100.
51. Grey to Asquith, 31 December 1908, F.O. 800/100. Doc. 46.
52. Hardinge to Bryce, Washington, 23 October 1908. Hardinge MSS. (1908).
53. Hardinge to the King, 26 March 1909, Hardinge MSS. (1909). Doc. 47.
54. Grey to Bryce, Washington, 25 December 1908, Bryce MSS., vol. 28. Doc. 48.
55. Hardinge to Nicolson, 30 March 1909, B.D.V. 807, n. 1.
56. Grey to Hardinge, 13 January 1909, Hardinge MSS. (1909).
57. Bridge, p. 231.
58. Grey was unable to persuade British financiers to float a loan to the new Government in September 1908, nor could he induce them to invest in Turkish enterprises. Platt, pp. 193–4, 210; Dakin, p. 404.
59. Lowther to Hardinge, 20 and 25 April 1909, F.O. 800/193. Doc. 49.
60. Hardinge to Nicolson, 12 May 1909, F.O. 800/342.
61. Hardinge to Villiers, 29 April 1909, Hardinge MSS. (1909).
62. Hardinge to Nicolson, 12 May 1909, F.O. 800/342.
63. Minto to Morley, 23 March 1908, Morley MSS., EUR. D. 573/14.
64. Chapman, pp. 83–5.
65. Hardinge to Lowther, 1 May 1909, F.O. 800/193.
66. Grey to Nicolson, 18 August 1910, F.O. 800/73. See Dakin, pp. 401–5.
67. Morley to Minto, 21 May 1909, Morley MSS., EUR. D. 573/4.
68. Chapman, pp. 104–10. Doc. 50.
69. Cartwright to Nicolson, 3 February 1911, F.O. 800/347.
70. Nicolson to Lowther, 6 February 1911, F.O. 800-193. Doc. 52.
71. Grey to Bertie, 18 January 1911, B.D.X. I, 654.
72. Spring, pp. 120–37; Kazemzadeh, pp. 594–7; Chapman, pp. 130–41.
73. Nicolson to Grey, 24 August 1910, F.O. 800/73.
74. Goschen to Hardinge, 28 March 1911, Hardinge MSS. (1911).
75. Hardinge to Nicolson, 24 August 1911, F.O. 800/350; Busch, pp. 322–30.
76. Busch, pp. 320–36; Chapman, pp. 139–48. Doc. 51.
77. See William C. Askew, *Europe and Italy's Acquisition of Libya, 1911–12* (North Carolina, 1942).
78. Hardinge to Nicolson, 15 October 1911, F.O. 800-351.
79. Grey to Nicolson, 23 September 1911, F.O. 800/350.
80. Churchill to Nicolson, 26 September 1911, B.D. IX. I, 240.
81. Doc. 53.
82. Nicolson to Findlay, Sofia, 18 October 1910, F.O. 800/344.
83. Grey to Nicolson, 1 October 1912, F.O. 800/358.

CHAPTER 4

1. S. F. Wells, Jr., 'British Strategic Withdrawal from the Western Hemisphere 1904–6', *Canadian Historical Journal* (1968), p. 351.
2. D. C. Watt, *Personalities and Policies* (London, 1965) pp. 22–9.

3. K. Bourne, *Britain and the Balance of Power in North America, 1815–1908* (London, 1967) pp. 302–29. The battleship strength of the U.S.A. stood at nine in 1897, twenty-seven built or building in 1909.
4. Wells, pp. 340, 348–56. For a slightly different approach see D. C. Gordon, *The Dominion Partnership in Imperial Defense, 1870–1914* (Baltimore, 1965) pp. 180–6.
5. J. A. S. Grenville, *Lord Salisbury and Foreign Policy* (London, 1964) pp. 54–73. H. C. Allen, *Great Britain and the United States 1783–1952* (London, 1954) pp. 523–39; A. E. Campbell, *Great Britain and the United States 1895–1903* (London, 1960).
6. Kimberley to Rosebery, 14 November 1896, quoted in Christopher Howard, *Splendid Isolation* (London, 1967) p. 13.
7. Grenville, pp. 199–217; C. S. Campbell, *Anglo-American Understanding, 1898–1903* (Baltimore, 1957); R. G. Neale, *Britain and American Imperialism 1898–1900* (Brisbane, 1965).
8. Bourne, p. 381.
9. See Chapter 2.
10. A. Tischendorff, *Great Britain and Mexico in the Era of Porfirio Diaz* (Durham, N.C., 1961); D. Young, *Member for Mexico: A Biography of Weetman Pearson, First Viscount Cowdray* (London, 1966); P. Calvert, *The Mexican Revolution 1910–1914* (Cambridge, 1968).
11. Except to appeal to the 'open door' when British trade or investments were threatened. As he summed up his lack of a policy in 1910, 'a strong position morally is not everything but it is not without some value'. Calvert, p. 35.
12. L. W. Martin, *Peace Without Victory* (New Haven, 1958) p. 21.

CHAPTER 5

1. I am grateful to R. Crampton of the University of Kent, who made a number of helpful suggestions on the draft of this section. Mr Crampton is writing a book on Anglo-German relations in the Near East, 1912–1914.
2. E. C. Helmreich, *The Diplomacy of the Balkan Wars, 1912–1913* (Cambridge, Mass., 1938) pp. 195–6; Taylor, *The Struggle for Mastery*, pp. 490–1.
3. Nicolson to Bertie, 11 October 1912, F.O. 800/165.
4. Cf. Lowe, I, p. 22.
5. Helmreich, pp. 166–7.
6. *Ibid.*, pp. 182–5; 189.
7. Nicolson to Lowther, 14 October 1912, F.O. 800/193.
8. Grey to Bertie, 30 October 1912, B.D. IX. II, 82.
9. A. J. P. Taylor, *The Struggle for Mastery*, pp. 492–3.
10. Nicolson to Lowther, 4 February 1913, F.O. 800/193.
11. Stamfordham to the King, 8 November 1912. Royal Archives, Geo.V. K. 404/10.
12. Lord Riddell, *More Pages from my Diary 1908–1914* (London, 1934) pp. 98–134.
13. Asquith to Grey, 4 November 1912, F.O. 800/100.
14. Asquith to the King, 7 November 1912, Cabinet Papers, Cab. 41/33/67.
15. Grey to Buchanan, desp. 393, 26 November 1912; to Goschen, desp. 302, 29 November 1912, B.D. IX. II, 283 and 310.
16. Nicolson to Goschen, 13 November 1912, F.O. 800/359.
17. Goschen to Nicolson, 25 November 1912, F.O. 800/360.
18. Nicolson to Hardinge, 21 November 1912, F.O. 800/360.

19. Helmreich, p. 245; Malcolm F. Carroll, *Germany and the Great Powers 1866–1914: A Study in Public Opinion and Foreign Policy* (New York, 1938) p. 727.
20. George V to Grey, 8 December 1912, Grey to George V, 9 December 1912, B.D.X. II, 452 and 453, Prince Henry wrote later to the King that 'Haldane had, in a conversation with our Ambassador (Lichnowsky) on the 6th of December . . . stated the fact point blanc (sic) officially from the point of Sir E. Grey. W[illiam] further mentioned that though this was felt as rather a blow, he would have to take the consequences.' Prince Henry of Prussia to King George V, 14 December 1912, Royal Archives, Geo. V. M. 520/2A.
21. Its members were Cambon (France), Grey (England), Imperiali (Italy), Lichnowsky (Germany), Mensdorff (Austria), and Benckendorff (Russia). Grey noted subsequently that Lichnowsky was not over-zealous in support of Austria's claims. Grey, I, p. 275.
22. *Ibid.*, p. 272.
23. Serbia was promised commercial access to the Adriatic instead.
24. Grey to Lloyd George, 21 December 1912, Lloyd George Papers, C/4/14/8.
25. Asquith to the King, 9 January 1913, Cab. 41/34/1.
26. Lowther to Nicolson, 30 January 1913, F.O. 800/193.
27. *Ibid.*, 13 March 1913.
28. Asquith to the King, 17 January 1913, Cab. 41/34/2.
29. Grey to Buchanan, private tel., 17 February 1913, B.D. IX. II, 626.
30. Grey to Buchanan, tel. 234, 17 March 1913, B.D. IX. II, 723.
31. Minute by Winston Churchill, 2 April 1913, Lloyd George Papers, C/3/15/21. Doc. 60.
32. Grey to Bertie, 3 April 1913, F.O. 800/161.
33. Asquith to the King, 3 April 1913, Cabinet papers, Cab. 41/34/12.
34. Grey to Buchanan, 3 May 1913, F.O. 800/161.
35. Grey to Cartwright, desp. 98, 1 May 1913, B.D. IX. II, 926.
36. Crewe to Hardinge, 4 September 1913, Hardinge MSS. (1913). Doc. 63.
37. The last meeting was held on 11 August 1913.
38. Grey, I, p. 265. Doc. 61.
39. Asquith to the King, 9 January 1913, Cab. 41/34/1.
40. Tyrrell to Spring-Rice, 30 July 1913, F.O. 800/241.
41. Hardinge to G. B. Allen, 18 June 1913, Hardinge MSS. (1913); Nicolson to Hardinge, 9 January 1913, F.O. 800/362.
42. Kiderlen-Waechter died at the end of December 1912.
43. Grey to Goschen, 7 November 1912, F.O. 800/62.
44. Grey to Rodd, 13 January 1913, B.D. X. II, 455.
45. Memorandum by Stamfordham, 25 May 1913, Royal Archives, Geo. V. M. 450/78. To calm French apprehension Grey insisted on the family nature of the visit. It also enabled him to excuse himself from accompanying the King to Berlin
46. Nicolson to Lowther, 19 February 1913, F.O. 800/193.
47. Steiner, pp. 147–52.
48. Hardinge to Chirol, 30 April 1913, Hardinge MSS. (1913).
49. Memorandum by Bertie, 23 June 1913, F.O. 800/161.
50. H. Lee to Bertie, 14 April 1914, F.O. 800/188.
51. Steiner, pp. 152–4.
52. See Collins, Chapter 3, pp. 100–25.
53. Harcourt to Grey, 8, 9 and 14 January 1914; Grey to Harcourt, 10 and 11 January 1914, F.O. 800/91. Docs 66, 67, 68, 69.
54. Minute by Churchill, 2 February 1913, on Rodd to Grey, 20 January 1913, F.O. 800/64.

55. E. L. Woodward, *Great Britain and the German Navy*, p. 431.
56. The Admiralty had adopted a standard of 60 per cent superiority in dread-noughts over Germany in 1912, Woodward, *Great Britain and the German Navy*, p. 367.
57. Churchill had first mentioned this proposal in 1912, *ibid.*, pp. 368–70.
58. *Ibid,*, pp. 417–21.
59. Grey to Churchill, 21 October 1913, F.O. 800/87.
60. Donald C. Gordon, *The Dominion Partnership in Imperial Defense, 1870–1914* (Baltimore, 1965) pp. 256–65.
61. They numbered McKenna, Harcourt, Beauchamp, Samuel, Simon, Runciman, Hobhouse and, probably, John Burns.
62. Woodward, *Great Britain and the German Navy*, pp. 391–4.
63. Memorandum by Lloyd George, December 1913, Cabinet Papers, Cab. 37/117/97. Doc. 64.
64. Memorandum by Churchill, 10 January 1914, Cabinet Papers, Cab. 37/118/6. Doc. 65.
65. For details see Randolph Churchill, *Winston S. Churchill*, II, pp. 655–86.
66. Quoted in Woodward, *Great Britain and the German Navy*, pp. 425–7.
67. Grey persuaded Churchill not to accept an invitation by the German Emperor to visit Kiel in the summer. The First Lord hoped to meet Tirpitz, and discuss naval questions with him. Grey pointed out that such a meeting would provoke too much speculation and alarm in Europe. Marder, *From the Dreadnought*, I, 311–77.
68. See pp. 51–2
69. Nicolson to Goschen, 7 April 1914, F.O. 800/373; Hardinge to Nicolson, 19 December 1912, F.O. 800/361.
70. Minute by Grey on A. Hardinge to Tilley, 5 February 1913, F.O. 800/71.
71. Lowe, I, pp. 217–22.
72. Willequet, p. 266.
73. Memorandum by Bertie, 19 February 1914, F.O. 800/188.
74. Bertie to Grey, 12 February 1914, B.D. X. II, 362.
75. Grey to Goschen, desp. 40, 13 June 1912, B.D. X. II, 337.
76. A. Hardinge to Crowe, 29 October 1912, F.O. 371/1741.
77. Goschen to Grey, desp. 172, 21 April 1914, B.D. X. II, 374.
78. See Willequet, pp. 267–9.
79. Bethmann Hollweg agreed on 27 July 1914 that the convention should be signed immediately and published in six months time. *Ibid.*, p. 269.
80. Nicolson to Goschen, 14 October 1913, F.O. 800/370.
81. Nicolson to Goschen, 4 November 1913, F.O. 800/370.
82. Nicolson to Goschen, 14 November 1913, F.O. 800/370.
83. Nicolson to Bunsen, 16 February 1914, F.O. 800/372.
84. Although the British believed that German influence in Constantinople was increasing, there is evidence of growing tension between Germany and Turkey after 1912. 'German diplomatic and financial circles had little confidence in the ability of the Ottoman Empire to survive, although they hoped that the final dissolution would be deferred as long as possible.' See H. S. W. Corrigan, 'German-Turkish Relations and the Outbreak of War in 1914: A Re-assessment', *Past and Present* (no. 36, 1967) pp. 144–52.
85. Grey to Nicolson, 12 April 1913, F.O. 800/365.
86. Mallet to Nicolson, 24 February 1914, F.O. 800/372.
87. Crewe to Hardinge, 21 August 1913, Hardinge MSS. (1913).
88. Asquith to the King, 10 July 1913, Cabinet Papers, Cab. 41/34/25. Doc. 62.
89. Platt, p. 216.

90. Grey to Mallet, 9 February 1914, B.D. X. I, 240.
91. Quoted in Callwell, I, p. 129.
92. O'Beirne to Grey, B.D. X. I, 385.
93. Mallet to Grey, 5 December 1913, B.D. X. I, 405.
94. Grey to Goschen, 2 January 1914, B.D. X. I, 457.
95. Chapman, pp. 141–204; Platt, pp. 214–17.
96. Marian Ruth Kent, 'British Government Interest in Middle East Oil Concessions, 1900–1925' (unpublished Ph.D. thesis, London, 1968) pp. 9–246.
97. Lamb, *The McMahon Line*, II, pp. 440–4.
98. *Ibid.*, pp. 444–8.
99. Crewe to Hardinge, 14 November 1913, Hardinge MSS. (1913).
100. Lamb, *The McMahon Line*, II, pp. 453–6.
101. Buchanan to Nicolson, 28 May 1914, F.O. 800/374.
102. Marian Jack, 'The Purchase of the British Government's Shares in the British Petroleum Company', *Past and Present* (no. 39, 1966) pp. 139–68.
103. Spring, pp. 316–28.
104. Lamb, *The McMahon Line*, II, pp. 620–5.
105. *Ibid.*, pp. 510–12.
106. Grey to Buchanan, 18 March 1914, B.D. X. I. 535.
107. Lamb, *The McMahon Line*, II, p. 514.
108. Nicolson to Buchanan, 14, 28 July 1914, B.D. X. II, Appendix I, p. 821. Doc. 59.
109. Minute by Grey, on George Graham (Paris) to Tyrrell, 26 January 1913, F.O. 800/54.
110. Grey to Bertie, 4 March 1913, F.O. 800/166.
111. Nicolson to Goschen, 11 March 1913, F.O. 800/364. Docs 70, 71.
112. Memorandum by Bertie, 23 June 1913, F.O. 800/166.
113. Marder, *From the Dreadnought*, I, pp. 309–10; Williamson, pp. 335–8. Doc. 73.
114. 'No such negotiations are in progress, and none are likely to be entered upon so far as I can judge. But, if any agreement were to be concluded that made it necessary to withdraw or modify the Prime Minister's statement of last year . . . it ought, in my opinion, to be and I suppose that it would be, laid before Parliament.' House of Commons, 11 June 1914, quoted in Grey, I, p. 289.
115. Memorandum by Bertie, 25 June 1914, F.O. 800/171.
116. Memorandum by Bertie, 16 July 1914, F.O. 800/161. Docs 72, 74, 75.
117. I am very grateful to Dr Cameron Hazlehurst of Nuffield College, Oxford, for suggestions and advice which greatly assisted me in the preparation of this section. See Dr Hazlehurst's book on the Cabinet and foreign policy in this period, *Politicians at War, July 1914–May 1915* (London, 1971).
118. Nicolson to Goschen, 5 May 1914, F.O. 800/374.
119. Luigi Albertini, *The Origins of the War of 1914* (Oxford, 1952–1957) i, pp. 1–257; Agatha Ramm, *Germany 1789–1919* (London, 1967) pp. 417–25; Fritz Fischer, *Germany's Aims in the First World War* (London, 1967) pp. 50–7.
120. Nicolson to Bunsen, 20 July 1914, F.O. 800/375.
121. Grey to Rumbold, Berlin, desp. 214, 6 July 1914, B.D. XI. 32.
122. Grey to Bunsen, 24 July 1914, B.D. XI. 91.
123. Minute by Crowe on Buchanan to Grey, 24 July 1914, B.D. XI. 101.
124. Steiner, p. 156.
125. Asquith to the King, 25 July 1914, quoted in Roy Jenkins, *Asquith* (London, 1964) p. 324.
126. Samuel to his mother, 26 July 1914, Samuel MSS., A./156. Samuel was at this time President of the Local Government Board.

127. Minute by Salisbury, undated, on memorandum by Lansdowne, 17 March 1902, Balfour MSS., no. 49730.
128. Asquith to the King, 30 July 1914, quoted in Jenkins, p. 325. Docs 30, 76.
129. As Hazlehurst shows, there were considerable differences in attitude between those Ministers as to the circumstances in which England might eventually become involved. Not all of them were opposed to British intervention in all circumstances. Samuel, for instance, played an ambiguous part throughout.
130. Memorandum by C. P. Scott, 27 July 1914, Scott MSS., no. 50901. Lloyd George also told Scott that he believed Germany would strike hard at France through Belgium, and then attack Russia.
131. Rough notes by Masterman, undated, Cabinet Notes, July–August 1914, Lloyd George papers, C/box/14.
132. Albertini, II, p. 502; Fischer, pp. 76–81.
133. Grey to Goschen, tel. 231, 30 July 1914, B.D. XI. 303.
134. Albertini, II, p. 540; see also G. Ritter, *The Schlieffen Plan* (London, 1958).
135. Jenkins, p. 327.
136. *Ibid.*, p. 327.
137. Villiers (Brussels) to Grey, 1 August 1914, B.D. XI. 395: The Belgian Foreign Minister then assured the British Minister that 'Belgium will to the utmost of her power maintain neutrality, and desires and expects other Powers to observe and uphold it,'
138. Villiers to Grey, 2 August 1914, B.D. XI. p. 476. Germany invaded Luxembourg on the 2nd.
139. Samuel to Mrs Samuel, 2 August 1914, Samuel MSS., A/157/697. Doc. 77.
140. Rough note by Harcourt, Cabinet Notes, 2(?) August 1914, Lloyd George papers, C/box/12.
141. Samuel to Mrs Samuel, 2 August 1914, see above.
142. Lloyd George, I. p. 43.
143. Samuel to Mrs Samuel, 2 August 1914, see above.
144. Memorandum by C. P. Scott, 3 and 4 September 1914, Scott MSS., 50901. Docs 78, 79.
145. Kenneth C. Morgan, *Wales in British Politics, 1868–1922* (Cardiff, 1964) p. 275, and *David Lloyd George, Welsh Radical as World Statesman* (Cardiff, 1963) p. 50.
146. Memorandum by C. P. Scott, 3 August 1914, Scott MSS., no. 50901.
147. Loreburn, pp. 3 ff.; Morley, pp. 17 ff.; Lloyd George, I, p. 58.
148. Albertini, III, pp. 517–22. For a recent discussion on the July crisis see J. Joll, 'The 1914 Debate Continues: Fritz Fischer and his Critics', *Past and Present* (no. 34, 1966) pp. 100–13; P. H. S. Hatton, 'Britain and Germany in 1914: The July Crisis and War Aims', and J. Michael Kitch, 'The Promise of the New Revisionism: A review of the *Journal of Contemporary History*, vol. 1, 3 (July 1966), on "1914"', *Past and Present* (no. 36, 1966) pp. 138–43; 153–65.
149. J. A. Spender to Herbert Samuel, 20 November 1941, Samuel MSS., A/45.
150. A. J. P. Taylor, *Struggle for Mastery*, p. 525.
151. W. N. Medlicott, *Contemporary England, 1914–1964* (London, 1967) pp. 11–12.
152. Memorandum by C. P. Scott, 3 August 1914, Scott MSS., no. 50901.

Index

Index

Index

of Duchy of Lancaster (1914–1915), 147, 153

Montagu, Edwin: Chancellor of Duchy of Lancaster (1915–16), 241; Minister for Munitions (1916), 246, 322; Secretary of State for India (1917–22), 365, 368

Mediterranean: and Anglo-French relations, 52–8; and Turkey, 91

Mensdorff, Count Albert von, Austro-Hungarian Ambassador to England (1904–14), 112, 113, 116, 266–7

Mesopotamia, (Iraq), 210–12, 214–19, 222, 357–8, 360–4, 377

Metternich Wolff, Count, German ambassador to England (1901–1912), 15, 21, 33–5, 41, 42, 50

Mexico, 102–6

Minto, Earl, Viceroy of India (1905–10), 63, 64, 87

Monroe Doctrine, 98, 99, 106

Montenegro, 95, 107, 110, 112–16

Morley, John (Viscount Morley of Blackburn): Secretary of State for India (1905–10), 32, 63–5, 88; Lord President of Council (1910–14), 36, 42–6, 54, 55, 74, 91, 135, 146, 150–2

Morocco, 8, 12–15, 21–4, 37–48, 71, 92

Neratov, A. A., Russian deputy Foreign Minister (1911), 71, 72, 90

Nicholas II, Emperor of Russia (1895–1917), 11, 64, 68, 80, 89, 118, 140, 149

Nicolson, Sir Arthur (Baron Carnock): British representative at Algeciras (1906), 23, 24; British ambassador to Russia (1906–1910), 20, 64, 65, 68, 84, 86, 89;

Permanent Under-Secretary, Foreign Office (1910–16), 36, 40, 49, 51, 52, 54, 56, 58, 66, 69, 70, 72, 73, 90–4, 109–11, 118–120, 124, 127–9, 133, 137, 138, 141, 143, 145, 149, 173, 210, 216, 217, 218, 235, 294

Oil, 102–6, 132, 136, 210, 213, 357, 364, 373

Palestine, 220–2, 225–6, 228–9, 230, 233, 358–64, 376–7; see also Syria; Husain

Panama canal, 100–2

Pauncefote, Sir Julian (Baron Pauncefote), British ambassador to U.S.A. (1889–1907), 100–1

Peacemaking: Austrian efforts, 256–8, 260, 267, 271; British objectives, 234–6, 238–50, 256–260, 261–74, 340–2, 346–8, 350–351, 358, 360, 365, 370, 373, 375–9; German objectives, 237, 252–6, 260–1, 265, 267–8, 309, 317; France and, 219–20, 234, 239, 257–8, 262, 264, 339, 342–346, 351, 353, 359–61, 367, 369; Italy and, 171–3, 179–80, 258–260, 264; Russia and, 234, 307–309, 315, 323–4, 329–32; see also Wilson, Woodrow

Pearson, Weetman D. (Viscount Cowdray), oil engineer, 102–6

Pease, J. A., President of Board of Education (1911–15), 146, 150

Persia, 48, 59–62, 64–76, 87, 89, 119, 133–8, 210, 330, 376, 378

Picot, François Georges, French diplomat, 218–19, 222, 224

Poincaré, Raymond, French premier (1912–13, 1922–4), President of France (1913–20), 53, 56–7,

Index